Great Cloud of Witnesses Speak:

Interviews with Martha, Lazarus, Thomas, and Timothy

Paul Nthoba
Matthew Robert Payne

Please visit *http://personal-prophecy-today.com* to sow into Matthew's writing ministry, to request a personal prophecy or life coaching, or to contact him.

Cover design by akira007 at fiverr.com.

Book design by WildBlu Design at *wendy@wildbludesign.com*.

Editing by Lisa Thompson at *www.writebylisa.com*. You can email Lisa at *writebylisa@gmail.com* for your editing needs.

Paperback ISBN: 978-1-925845-03-7

First Edition: August 2018

0 1 2 3 4 5 6 7 8 9 10

Dedication

To my son, Brandyn:

Some of my best memories include my son, Brandyn. I have only seen my son once in the last seventeen years, but I have great love for him. From his Facebook posts, I can see that he is growing up to become a caring and intelligent young man.

I love you Brandyn.

Introduction

Some years ago, I recorded the interviews with nineteen saints from heaven and produced a book called *Great Cloud of Witnesses Speak.* Due to pressure from other Christians, I took down the original YouTube videos that I used to produce that book. That book has gone on to be loved by many people, which has encouraged me to do other interviews with saints. Shortly after I took down those videos, I did another series of interviews that I planned to make into another book.

I never got around to producing another book, but my coauthor, Paul, came across the videos and loved them. He asked me if he could type up four of his favorite interviews, and we decided to compile this book. It was largely created by Paul, who faithfully transcribed the videos and then lovingly added his commentary at the end of each section. I pray that as you read this book, that you too are blessed like Paul was and that you are taken to another place and time.

TABLE OF CONTENTS

Interview with Martha

❖ Introduction

Hello, this is Matthew Robert Payne, and this will be an interview with Martha. I also supplied the questions that I will be asking.

I welcome Martha. I pray that the Holy Spirit would give her the answers to the questions and that she would convey those answers to me. And I pray that you would be blessed by both the questions and the answers that Martha delivers to me.

For those who aren't watching, Martha is seated on my couch, and as I ask each question, she will directly answer me just as the Holy Spirit speaks. She will give the answers directly to me because you can't hear her speaking. I will then share her answers as we go.

Question 1:

Martha, you are mentioned in the Bible as the sister of Mary and Lazarus. Can you tell us a little bit more about your family and your parents? Did you have any other sisters and brothers, and why did you live together like that?

Lazarus was my brother. We had kind parents that aren't mentioned in the Bible, but it was common in those days for sisters and brothers to live together, even after their parents died. At times, even a married brother still had his sisters living with him. In those days, families commonly lived together, and so did siblings. Our family consisted of Mary, Martha, and Lazarus and our parents. We had no other siblings.

In this way, Jesus knew us and became our dear friend. We had a tremendous relationship with Jesus. He used to come to our house and just let his hair down and relax with us. In the interview with Lazarus, Lazarus gave plenty of information about Jesus and about his interactions with us as a family.

Question 2:

You and your sister Mary seem to have had

different personalities. How did you get along with each other when you were growing up?

In Luke 10:38–42, the Bible mentions that Jesus was at our house and that he was teaching. To paraphrase the story, I was upset, and I came out to Jesus and asked, "Don't you care that Mary isn't helping me serve the food? Can you ask Mary to come and help me with the preparations in the kitchen?"

Jesus answered something like, "Mary has chosen a better thing to sit at my feet and listen to me. And that won't be taken away from her." From that interaction, through the years, people have recognized that we both had different personalities.

Mary was rare. In fact, it was traditional for the woman of the house to prepare food for the guests. A woman did not regularly sit down and listen to a rabbi when there was food to be prepared. Mary was doing something that was not customary, which was certainly rare.

When I made that appeal to Jesus, I fully expected Jesus to tell Mary, "Yeah, go in the kitchen, Mary, and help your sister. When we've eaten dinner and when you've finished cleaning up, you're quite welcome to sit down with me and listen then. But go and do your duties now." If I didn't expect Jesus to say that to my sister, if I hadn't known that Jesus would say what he did, I wouldn't have gone out there and requested that Jesus admonish her. Mary was being different and doing what wasn't customary. So from that story, people have the opinion that Mary and I were different.

We were different like any sisters or any siblings. Each person has their own unique personality. Numerous women have seen themselves like Mary—devoted to the worship of Jesus and sitting at his feet. Other women see themselves like Martha—busy doing things, doing the work of the ministry, and doing things for God. They find their fulfillment in being busy. This is an overgeneralization of who we are, and it takes more out of the story and more out of the context of the story than what is really there.

People would assume from this interaction, this biblical story, that I wasn't devoted to Jesus and that I didn't love Jesus for who he was. People assume that I wasn't into Jesus as much as Mary was into Jesus. While that might have some merit to it from the face of that story, I learned a lesson from that interaction with Jesus. Later after the meal, Jesus addressed the situation in more detail with me. I became a lot more relaxed around Jesus, and I was more devoted from that day on. But a kind rebuke always brings favor and brings change in a person's life. Jesus was kind in how he treated me and shared with me.

He was very generous to Mary, my sister. Mary and Jesus always had a close relationship. Lazarus had a close relationship with Jesus. Everyone in our family was really good friends with

Jesus. We were pretty special to him. We were pretty special to him.

Question 3:

How was your relationship with Lazarus? How was his relationship with Mary?

I had an older brother, Lazarus, and he was a tremendous brother to me. We shared the same parents and a common love for the God of Israel. We had a deep abiding love for the God of Israel. We recognized Jesus as the Messiah, and he shared with us that he was the chosen one of God and the chosen one to lead Israel in the future. We understood that he was a loving teacher and a miracle worker. He did miracles. He raised Lazarus from the dead. But Jesus was just a very personal friend of ours.

To get back to the question, Lazarus was a great brother to have. We owned a property, and we had workers there, servants that served us. We had quite a profitable farm; you might call it a farm or a ranch where you live. But we had a successful business. We looked up to Lazarus. He had a lot of love in him.

Mary was a real romantic. She was desperately in love with Jesus. Jesus was everything. Many women on earth now come to know Jesus through the Bible, and they come to know him better when they talk back and forth with him. Many women in my day wanted to marry Jesus if they would have been given the opportunity. They would have married him without hesitation. Mary was that kind of girl. She had a tremendous love and devotion for Jesus. She worshipped him.

She continues to worship him here in heaven. She hangs on his every word. I don't know if you've ever come across this kind of teacher on earth. I'm not sure, listeners, if you've ever come across a teacher on earth where you hang on every word they say, and you are essentially almost addicted to their words and to their sermons. It is quite rare for someone to be so anointed that you can hang on every word that they say so that you are intoxicated by the person's preaching. Jesus was that sort of person. He could talk about any subject, and you'd be fascinated with what he had to say. Mary was absolutely devoted to Jesus.

John 12:1–11 says that she anointed him before he died. They said that the perfume could have been sold, and the money given to the poor and used to feed many people. The perfume could have been sold, and the revenue from the perfume could have been given to the poor. But Jesus said that Mary's name would be remembered and preached about in the future. She would be remembered for generations to come because of her devotion to him. Mary was truly special, and she did have a more intimate love for Jesus.

I loved Jesus as well, but we are all different kinds of people. I was practical, and I did have love in my heart for Jesus. But something was missing with Mary. She missed our parents, especially our mother, and she had this emotional need in her life. She had a gap, the type that all people seem to have in their hearts, a God-shaped gap. Jesus came along, and he totally filled that gap in her life. She was like a little lamb that follows its mother around or a young baby lion, following its mother around. She was like a tiny baby, suckling on its mother, like Jesus was a mother. It was a beautiful sight to see.

Lazarus was a protective older brother. He spoke the truth and wasn't afraid of being honest. He really respected Jesus and had a lot of love for him. He loved Jesus as a teacher and as a rabbi, but he wasn't overly awed by Jesus. He wasn't completely infatuated with Jesus or totally in awe of him. He was more down to earth, and he related to Jesus as a brother. Jesus really loved that. Jesus was used to crowds following him, worshipping him, and hanging onto his every word. My brother, Lazarus, just had a great friendship with Jesus and treated him normally. It wasn't like Lazarus was worshipping Jesus, but he was treating him as an equal, like a brother, and Jesus really loved that.

Some people who are really popular in the world's eyes, such as Michael Jackson or Lady Diana, can't lead a normal life. They had lots of fans. For example, Michael Jackson had many loyal fans. He couldn't meet anyone that wasn't overly in awe of him. They all treated him like royalty and looked up to him. In a way, they sucked up to him. It's hard for people who are very popular to have a regular conversation with someone so that the person treats them like an equal and not as someone special.

Lazarus had that kind of relationship with Jesus. He respected and honored Jesus, but he didn't treat him like a Lazarus had that kind of relationship with Jesus. He respected and honored Jesus, but he didn't treat him like a superstar. He treated him like a brother, like an equal.

People who are used to the adoration of others really respect a person when they can just relax, let their hair down, and not have to impress the other person. They can simply be themselves when they're together. Whenever Jesus was at our house, he had the openness and the ability just to relax and even to talk about some of the hassles and challenges he was having in his travels. He could speak of the things that were annoying him and getting him down, and he could freely express himself. I hope that I covered much of what you wanted to hear.

Question 4:

The Bible mentions in Luke 10:38–42 that Jesus spoke up for Mary when you were working hard and she was sitting and listening. How did you feel about this, and

did Jesus compliment or encourage you as well?

Yes, we covered that initially. But Matthew wasn't aware that this question was coming up. When I told Jesus to ask Mary to come and help me in the kitchen, that was just one of many conversations that Jesus and I had. I knew that the boundaries were clear. I could even call to Jesus to come to the kitchen and share while sitting nearby so that I could listen while preparing the food. Jesus understood that. I asked him to come near the kitchen on several occasions so that he could share what he was saying while I continued to prepare food and listened to him. Jesus really respected that. I was compromising as it was always my duty to prepare and serve the food for Jesus. He didn't mind standing outside while I was preparing the food. He spoke more loudly so that I could listen while I worked.

Mary was never distracted from that day on by preparing food. But when Jesus decided to stand next to the kitchen and share his teachings, Mary came into the kitchen and helped me prepare. She could then listen as we both worked together. Mary just wanted to listen. If you've ever heard Jesus speak, he's amazing to listen to, and you don't want anything to distract you while you listen. Jesus had many amazing things to say to me. listen to, and you don't want anything to distract you while you listen. Jesus had many amazing things to say to me.

If you know Jesus personally, if you have a relationship with him where he regularly talks with you, you'll find that he's always telling you your good points and regularly encouraging you. He frequently says that he's proud of you. Jesus and the Father must have told Matthew that they love him and that they are proud of him two to three hundred times. Matthew has been told that he is loved at least two hundred times. He's been told that they are proud of him at least a hundred times. He has been told in prophecy that he is very humble at least fifty times.

Whenever Jesus is around, he is encouraging. This is one of his key characteristics. It's impossible to have a relationship with Jesus for any amount of time without being encouraged by him. Jesus was such an encourager.

That story in the Bible is just one of many encounters we had with Jesus. He really admired the fact that I was studious. He admired the fact that I wanted to prepare the food and get things ready. It was just motherly of me. I was just doing my womanly duties, and he respected and honored that in me. That's why he came out to the kitchen and spoke, and I was able to listen to him as I prepared the food. A lesser person wouldn't do that if they thought a lot of themselves. They would stay in the living room and speak there instead. But Jesus came out to the kitchen, knowing that I was torn between preparing food and listening to him. After that first occasion, I compromised; he came out and stood near the kitchen and spoke loudly so that I could listen as I prepared the food. Once Mary realized that she could hear also, she came alongside me, and we prepared food and did the work twice as quickly, and everything was served.

You can only find out these types of details through an interview or by talking to a saint. Not everything that happened is spelled out in the Bible. John, one of the disciples, said in his book that if everything had been recorded, if everything were written down that happened with Jesus, everything he said and did, the world couldn't contain the books. (See John 21:25.) That is true of Jesus. So this is a little additional insight into him.

Question 5:

Many women on earth relate to you, Martha. They feel guilty that they are not like Mary. Is there anything that you can tell those women to encourage them to be happy with how God created them for his purpose in a beautiful way?

Yes, that story has impacted many women whenever they read it in the Bible or even when they listen to preachers talk about it. No story in the Bible should make you feel condemned or guilty. A lot of guilt and condemnation goes along with that story. Believe me, Mary was an exception to the rule. If many women were together in that day and they saw the actions of Mary, Mary would have been the one in trouble because she wasn't living up to the normal expectations of the day. She was being very disrespectful to her sister by neglecting her duties.

But Jesus always came and challenged what people did. He challenged the culture of the day. That's why Jesus asked the woman at the well, the Samaritan woman, for some water. (See John 4.) Not only was he not supposed to speak to a woman who was alone, but she was a Samaritan, and Jews didn't speak to them at all. He broke both the cultural rule of not speaking to a single woman and of not speaking to a Samaritan. He broke two rules or traditions of that day. Jesus was a rule-breaker.

Mary responded to Jesus and changed her custom and what was expected of her when she sat down at the feet of Jesus. I was just listening to him as I worked. She wanted to listen to Jesus more than she wanted to do what was expected of her. I was the normal person who acted in accordance with the cultural expectations of the day. I didn't neglect my duties. I think my response was wrongly portrayed for generations. Because of that, many women have felt guilty for being all about being busy and doing things. Very little, if anything, can be done when people just sit on the floor and listen all day.

Sometimes offerings have to be collected. Someone has to sweep the church; someone has got to vacuum the carpet. Someone has to turn on the lights. Someone has to put out the flowers in the church. Someone has to steward the people in the church. The church has many roles to fill. Someone has to play the music. Someone has to sing. People can't just sit on the floor and do nothing. Many women and men out there feel inclined to be active and to serve. God is happy with their gifts and has gifted them to serve and to be respected and to be loved for what they are doing. There's a time for people to serve. Sometimes there's a time for them to be quiet and seated at the feet of Jesus and meditate with him.

Some people aren't happy unless they're busy. That's how they are made. They shouldn't be discouraged by that. That's why Jesus came and spoke near the kitchen so that I could have the best of both worlds. If I had to choose to be in the living room, listening to Jesus or in the kitchen preparing food and not listening, I couldn't neglect my duty. So I'd have to miss out on that more intimate time that Mary had with Jesus so that she formed a closer bond with him. Anyone who spends a lot of time with Jesus like Matthew does develops an intimate relationship with him that's not wasted. I want you to know that you can be busy and you can like action and have a job to do. In all this, you can still serve Jesus and be close to him. There's nothing wrong with praying or worshipping while you work. You can develop a close relationship with Jesus even while you are busy serving him.

I just want to encourage you that many kinds of people make up this world. Jesus wants you to use your gifts and do what comes naturally to you. He doesn't need the whole world sitting at his feet, worshipping him all the time. There's work to be done. Sometimes the world needs people who will work. Many times, in churches, only a small percentage of the people do nearly all the work. Some pastors wish that everyone would be like Martha and work and stay busy. But the fact of the matter is that most churches only have a few people doing the majority of the work. I hope that was encouraging to you.

Question 6:

Jesus seemed to spend his last days on earth staying with you and going on day trips to Jerusalem. Am I correct? Did you sense any seriousness and sadness arising in Jesus? Were you there when he rode on the donkey into Jerusalem?

Jesus did spend a lot of time with us. We lived close to Jerusalem, like it says in the Bible. He used to come to our place to hang out and let his hair down, like Lazarus said. We didn't see him when he rode into Jerusalem. But we did sense a shift, especially after he raised Lazarus from the dead. There was a change in Jesus. We sensed that he was approaching the time when he was going to be crucified. He told his disciples about the fact that he would be crucified. They didn't understand, but we knew that there was a heaviness about Jesus. He was starting to feel a greater burden as the day approached. We were very proud of Jesus, and we loved him with all of our hearts. He was very special to us. We created a safe haven for him to come and spend time at our place. He used to enjoy visiting us and letting his hair down, like I've said. He was tremendously at peace when he was at our place.

Question 7:

Were you there when Jesus was crucified? It must have been so awful.

Lazarus spoke about this. We did witness his crucifixion. Not everyone that knew Jesus or that was close to Jesus was mentioned in the Gospel accounts as being at the foot of the cross. Mary, Jesus's mother was mentioned, along with Mary Magdalene and John. But no one in our family—Lazarus, Mary, and Martha—was mentioned. I was tremendously saddened by what was happening to Jesus. He was even beaten when he got to the cross. He looked awful. Even if they hadn't crucified Jesus, he would have bled out and died from the whipping that he received, the horrific punishment that they gave him. His face was about twice the size of a normal face; it was so bruised, scarred, and beaten. It was horrific.

In Lazarus's interview, you will hear more about how Jesus looked. But it was just terrible to see what he went through. He told us that he was going to rise again, and Lazarus understood what he was saying. Even though we'd been told that he would rise again, it was horrific to see what he went through and what he suffered. He did that for mankind. He did that so that mankind could be saved and brought into a relationship with his Father and so that the Holy Spirit could come and live within the people who believe in Jesus. God wanted to come and inhabit people's lives so building of God. (See 1 Peter 2:5.)

He needed to win the power over sin. He paid a high price for the punishment for sin. Romans 6:23 says, "For the wages of sin is death; but the gift of God is eternal life through Jesus Christ our Lord" (KJV). Death had to be paid for the remission of sins, and Jesus provided that sacrifice for sin. (See Luke 24:47.) People could then become Christians, confess their sins to God, and be washed clean of sin. The guilt and condemnation of sin could be washed away, and people could have peace in their lives because of Jesus's death. It was a terrible thing to witness, but even more so because we weren't just his followers; we were his personal friends. It was heart-wrenching for us.

Did you meet Jesus on earth after he rose again?

Yes, we did see Jesus when he rose again. He came and visited us at the house, and we saw him and interacted with him. He spent a lot of time with his disciples, but he did come and visit us too. Of course, that isn't mentioned in the Bible, but we were witnesses to his resurrection. We were happy to meet him and see him again. His disciples came out and visited us, and Jesus was with them. That was such a joyful time. At first, he seemed like a ghost. Some people call it a ghost, but we saw a person who was dead alive again.

We saw him eat, and we saw the food go into his body and stay there. It is said that he had a resurrected body that could pass through walls. But he also could eat, and the food would stay in him without falling out. That was good to see. As saints, we aren't just a figment of Matthew's imagination. We are living just like Jesus is, and we can appear too and speak just like Jesus spoke. Jesus was the firstborn of a new creation, and we all live and exist in heaven.

Question 8:

How did you know Jesus's family: his mother, Mary; his sisters; and his brothers? What do you know about his father, Joseph?

We never knew Joseph, but we did know of Jesus's mother, Mary. She traveled with him over the years, halfway through his ministry. Mary Magdalene also used to travel with him. But the rest of his family didn't travel with him. We knew of his family, and we'd met them, but we mostly spent time with Jesus when he traveled. He used to visit us, and we did meet Mary. She was really loving and very humble. She couldn't ever come to grips with the fact that her son was to be a leader in Israel and be as popular as he was. She was like any mother with a son. She didn't expect the whole nation to be turned upside down by her son. This was so special to her. She never fully came to grips with it.

She was at the foot of the cross and saw her son in such a state, beaten and crucified. She was in tears, very sorrowful, which was so sad to see. We were friends with her. Joseph had died by the time Jesus was in ministry. Jesus's family was special to us, and we were special to him. The bond continued through many years to come. Many years after Jesus was resurrected and after he left to go to heaven in the ascension, we knew her family. We knew Mary and met his brothers and sisters, especially James, who had a big role in Jerusalem. We got to know James fairly well as the years progressed, and we used to visit him at the church in Jerusalem.

Question 9:

What was your role following the anointing of the Holy Spirit?

I was just a sister, just a sister. I didn't have a special role. My sister, Mary, was more anointed than I was. We were just followers of Jesus. We were simple people. I want you to know that not just pastors, prophets, apostles, evangelists, or teachers are special to Jesus. Every one of his followers is special to him. We're all special, and you don't have to have a special anointing or calling on your life or be in full-time ministry to be loved and used by Jesus. Ordinary people need others to come alongside them and share their faith with them and have an influence.

We started a house church in our home. People visited from Jerusalem, and they led our house church. Our community grew to up to about forty people in our house, including visitors. The house churches of those days were similar to a house church today. Everyone took on the role of a pastor, and everyone had their own role to play. Everyone was given a gift, or they flowed in the gifts of prophecy and could hear from Jesus. Many people were gifted in healing. We had quite a fellowship in our house church. I could hear from Jesus; I could prophesy. I wasn't a prophet, but I had a gift of prophecy. Mary was prophetic, and she was almost a prophet. But she was a really special woman, and she became a mystic.

Mary was a deep person with a deeply spiritual life. She grew and grew and grew and became deeper and deeper. She took on a teaching role in our house church. Many times, she led a service and taught. She had direct communication with the Holy Spirit and Jesus and received many insights from God and shared them with others. The people were very encouraged because the fresh manna was coming down from heaven through Mary. I was especially proud of her; it was time for me to sit at Mary's feet. I loved having a sister who was so turned on to Jesus. I was—and am still—just an average person. I deeply loved Jesus and am loved and respected in heaven, and I enjoy myself.

Question 10:

Is there anything you want to emphasize or tell us about our lives as Christians at this time?

I do have one thing that I want to tell you that Matthew also harps about in his books. It's just because it's so important. Take a spiritual gifts test and also do a Myers & Briggs analysis. Myers & Briggs is a temperament analysis. Find out who you are and what you are gifted in. Start to walk in your gifts and start to exercise them. Few things are more important than knowing what you are here to do and doing it.

Many Christians have no idea why they are here. They don't know what their purpose is, which is so sad. Don't let that be you. Make sure that you find out what you are called to do and why you are here. Start to walk that out.

You might not have an immediate opportunity to preach or to do what you are called to do. But if you seek God and if you obey him, you will learn to listen, which is important. You need the ability to hear from God. If you start to hear from God, listen to

God, and walk obediently, then God will open up the doors for you to do what you are meant to do. Find out your purpose and live it out. God didn't create you to sit on the sidelines. God didn't create you just to be a spectator. Some people are spectators in life, and others like me weren't tremendously empowered or used, but I had an effective role. I was the sister of Mary, who went on and did great things.

I encouraged my sister, Mary, and I was there for her. She could always talk to me, and we were always close. But even the average Christian without a big role in the Christian church can be an effective witness. You can be an effective witness for Jesus. You can be an example of his love to all those around you. You can be reviled and picked on and turn around in love and forgiveness toward those who have hurt you. You can meet people who are harsh and abrasive, and you can treat them with respect and love. You can feed the poor and give them money. You can do many things to witness effectively. You don't have to be anyone special.

Matthew isn't anyone special; he just has a close relationship with Jesus, with the Father, and with the Holy Spirit. He knows each of them intimately. And he persisted and used his gifts to do what God has called him to do. But one day, he might be well-known. At the moment, he's just doing what he is called to do. That's all God asks of you. All he wants from you is to find out what you are gifted to do and do that for the glory of Jesus. I'd encourage you to do that. Find out why you are here and start to live that out. You can find out more in Matthew's book, *Finding Your Purpose in Christ*.

It's very interesting to be here. I was interviewed once by Matthew in his first book, *Great Cloud of Witnesses Speak*, and this is the second interview that I've done with him. I hope that you were encouraged and that you learned some things in this interview. Don't be too hard on yourself. Remember that Jesus loves you for who you are. He created you to be you. He didn't create you to be anyone else; he didn't create you to be like anyone else. The only person you should be like is Jesus. The Apostle Paul said in 1 Corinthians 11:1, "Imitate me, just as I also imitate Christ." I encourage you to strive to be more like Jesus. Learn how to abide in Jesus and walk hand in hand with him. Then go and bless the world you live in.

Paul's Comments

This interview was great, and I learned a lot from it. Martha has such a humble personality. She is soft-spoken, gentle, and easygoing. I love how simply she explained herself in every answer. She tackled every question with the right answers. No answer was ambiguous, and she did not leave us hanging. She elaborated the answers with clarity and emphasized similar points and stuck to the theme. This interview was truly led by the Holy Spirit, which is what I picked up from the video of the interview.

Jesus was friends with Martha, Mary, and Lazarus, who all

came from one family. These siblings lived together as adults. Jesus could visit them any time, relax, and be himself. I believe Jesus found love and comfort in this family because they were such a close family. They loved to host people who came to their house to hear Jesus speak. Martha prepared food for them, and sometimes Mary helped too. This family loved people and opened their house to strangers. In Matthew 25:35, Jesus says, "For I was hungry, and you fed me. I was thirsty, and you gave me a drink. I was a stranger, and you invited me into your home" (NLT).

This family was open to a point that the Messiah, Jesus Christ, befriended them. We even learn later that their house eventually became a house church. I hope this encourages you to open your house to people. I believe it starts with your heart as you love people and give to others. This character attracts Jesus, which is why Jesus was friends with this family. If you struggle with this, pray and ask Jesus to help you love people and become a giver or a person who loves to share. As you start to walk in more love, the presence of Jesus will be felt in your home and around you.

Martha also addressed the issue of personality or character comparison. Most people compare themselves with others. I love the fact that Martha addressed this issue as she and Mary had been so often compared to each other by scholars and theologians throughout the years. She acknowledged their differences but highlighted that she was close to Jesus as well. She and Mary were wired differently. When she wanted Mary to come and help in the kitchen, she was being herself. Mary was also being herself by wanting to stay at the feet of Jesus. Therefore, this addresses a very important topic: people should know their gifts and not compare themselves to anyone else. They should still pursue Jesus through their gift.

What stood out the most to me in this interview is knowing our gifts and flowing in them to serve Jesus and becoming close to him. Jesus loves us the way we are. The perfect example was with Lazarus as Martha mentioned how he related to Jesus. Lazarus made it easy for Jesus to relax around him. For example, he didn't revere Jesus to the point of a superstar, and he didn't worship every step that Jesus took. He revered him, of course, but from the heart. He related to Jesus through simple friendship. Perhaps Jesus wants that from you. He wants to let his hair down when he visits you during your quiet times. He wants you to talk about anything and ask him anything. He wants to laugh and joke with you. Don't be too serious around him all the time, because you might be making him uncomfortable around you. Then he might rush out to leave the way that celebrities walk off the red carpet after a few photographs. Make him feel at home around you. (See Ephesians 3:17.) I hope that your relationship with Jesus will change for the better after reading this. Thank you.

Interview with Lazarus

❖ *Introduction*

Hello, this is Matthew Robert Payne, and this will be an interview with Lazarus, Jesus's friend. I have a hard time saying Lazarus. I am not sure if I am the only one in the world. I'm just sitting here; I am freshly shaven, I think I cut myself a couple of times. If you are watching the video clip, you might be able to see a bit of blood. It's interesting that I am bleeding a little on camera. But I am just here with Lazarus.

Many times, when the saints come down, I just interview the saints, and I leave it. I don't actually get to spend a lot of time with the saints and talk to them. I seem to quickly finish the interview and pack up and upload it and then go from there. I don't seem to interact much with the saints.

I just want to let you know that this is enjoyable for me. I enjoy listening to them, but for a full appreciation of their answers and what they say, I really need to listen to each interview again.

They speak through me, and I do hear what comes from my mouth, but I don't formulate the words that I say. They speak to me, and I have to find an English word for them. They say things, and I might not fully understand some of what they say before they say it. It's interesting for me too. I am not an expert. Since my friend Julie has been formulating the questions, I definitely can't make up the answers.

I've needed the saints to come and physically sit here and give me the answers to the questions. Only the saints or Jesus would know many of these answers. I hope that gives you a little bit of understanding and clears it up for you.

Welcome, Lazarus. I'm happy to say that Mary and Martha are here too. They are sitting and holding hands with Lazarus. He's happy to be here. That's good. I wish you could see them over on the couch, waving.

Question 1:

Lazarus, can you please tell us about your life? What were you doing before your death, and what caused your death?

I owned property and land. I farmed a bit. That's what I was doing with my life. I was fortunate to know Jesus as he was a part of my life. He often stopped in and visited me as he traveled through Jerusalem. We were very close. I got a very severe strain of pneumonia, and I wasn't going to recover. That's when they sent out warnings to Jesus. Hospitals can treat pneumonia now. Back then, it was a lot more serious, and there were complications. So my organs shut down. That's the answer to question one. That's why I died. Modern medicine can usually handle it now. But certainly back then, it was hard. I didn't die of cancer or anything like that.

Question 2:

Lazarus, when you were dead for four days in the tomb, where was your spirit?

Everyone who died—those who believed in Jesus or who followed the law and who were in God's good graces—went to Paradise. Jesus told the parable of the rich man. Apparently Lazarus, the poor man, went to Paradise, and he was in what they called Abraham's bosom. This was a separate place under the earth, which was also called Paradise. A chasm separated Hades from Paradise. You couldn't cross over between the two places. The people who had no chance went to Hades, and the people who had a chance of going to heaven one day went to Paradise. I was in Paradise, and I was quite happy there.

I heard, "Come forth," in the tomb. And then I came out. It

is interesting. Matthew heard several preachers teach on this, and I

I heard, "Come forth," in the tomb. And then I came out. It is interesting. Matthew heard several preachers teach on this, and I will share it here. The Jews had a belief that a person could be raised from the dead. Up until the third day, the spirit hovered around the body, but on the fourth day, the Jews believed that the spirit departed from the body to Hades or Paradise so that it was impossible to be raised from the dead. Jesus actually delayed his coming to me to make sure that he came on the fourth day. In this way, he wanted to emphasize the Jewish understanding that said it was impossible to come back from the dead after the third day. Jesus made sure he delayed his arrival until the fourth day to create a mighty sign and wonder for the Jews. He did a miracle that they had never seen done before. There was a specific reason that he waited for four days—not just two or three days. He wanted my resurrection to be a great sign. He also obeyed the Father in this as a precursor and sign of his own death.

Question 3:

What did you think just before you died? Did you believe that Jesus would come and heal you, or did you believe that even if you died, he'd raise you up?

I loved Jesus. He was his own man. I felt fortunate that he popped in and saw me from time to time when he was in ministry. I saw him regularly in his earlier years, but at times when he was ministering, he used to stop by and use our house as a place of respite to rest and relax. Martha and Mary waited on him and served him food. He just relaxed and prayed, talked to his disciples, and spent time with us. He let his hair down. Our home was a place of relaxation for him.

I knew that Jesus was busy. If he could have come to see me sooner, I thought that he would come. But I didn't know that he would do that sign and wonder. I had to die so that more people would believe in Jesus when he raised me from the dead. In my mind, I knew how sick I was. I accepted my death. I knew that Jesus could raise me. But I wasn't expecting him to.

I would compare it to growing up with a famous preacher who went to your church. Whenever he came back to your city, he came to your church and went out for coffee or dinner with you. He spent time with you whenever he was in town. He was an international preacher with a busy schedule. But whenever he was in your city when church was happening, he'd come to your church and go out for coffee or a meal with you. You'd feel really important. If a person like that spent time with you, you'd feel really special. That's how I felt about Jesus.

I made no demands on his time. We just lived to give him a respite, to help him relax. I will tell you this about Jesus: he found it hard to relax. He was always about his Father's business. Even when he was relaxing, he was fascinating to listen to as he shared stories of what he was doing in ministry. He told story after story, but interwoven in each story was a theme and a teaching. He was always teaching in themes. That's why Mary was so compelled to sit at his feet because she was just fascinated by his teachings.

I had no idea that he was going to resurrect me. It would be strange to know that you were dying but that you would be raised from the dead again. I had no idea what would happen until I heard my name called forth from the tomb. I had no idea that I would be healed and rise from the dead.

Question 4:

They say that you never smiled after Jesus resurrected you. Can you tell us why?

First of all, I was a close friend of Jesus, one of his best friends. I had a reason to smile while Jesus was alive. Some people taught history and created their own ideas about this. They were not well-informed. Matthew isn't even sure where Julie heard this, possibly from a commentary or other study material. I am obviously not telling Matthew where she heard this. People are allowed to be wrong when they write history; they don't have to be right.

Certainly I was joyful that I was alive again. It was wonderful to see my sisters again and see the impact that the early church made on the Jewish society. I was living in exciting times, and I lived for another fifteen years after I was raised from the dead. I lived to a ripe old age. I lived to see and experience time with some of the disciples as they used to stop in and see me and my family.

It's not true that I didn't smile. I witnessed the birth of the early church, the greatest time in history. I had plenty of reasons to be full of joy. I really knew some of the insiders and Jesus's inner circle of disciples. I have no idea why anyone would think that I never smiled again. That would imply that I was upset that I was raised from the dead, upset that I was alive. It's a relevant question, but I'm certainly glad to speak up today and put that theory and accusation to rest.

Question 5:

Lazarus, what did you do when Jesus left after he raised you from the dead and went into the wilderness called Ephraim? He went there because the Sanhedrin and the Pharisees sought to kill him. They even threatened to kill you, because your resurrection made many Jews believe in Jesus.

I went back to my farming life. I had work to do. Much of the work around my property really needed a man to do it. Even though I had servants, I needed to be in charge. Men respond to women who lead and who are in charge. But men like to respond to men. I got up and went back to work.

Jesus was fine. He did tell us that he wasn't going to meet a pleasant end. We understood that. His disciples didn't seem to want to accept that. Sometimes people wonder how his disciples didn't understand that he would die. You have to understand that they invested their whole lives in Jesus. They saw a future for themselves in Jesus's ministry. If Jesus became the Messiah and a ruler, the ruler over the nation, and dispelled the Romans, they were going to have positions of importance.

Sometimes we aren't really listening to what another person is saying. I was just Jesus's friend. I was a mate of Jesus, to use an Australian term. I was his close friend. I had no vested interest in Jesus living and becoming the ruler over the nation where we lived. When Jesus confessed to me that he would die too, raising me from the dead was really the nail in his coffin. It signified his death. I could receive it, and I knew what would happen.

He promised me that the Holy Spirit would come, that we would have visitations, and that I would see the early church start to arise. I would see the glory that he would bring his Father with his resurrection, his ascension to heaven, and the coming of the

Holy Spirit. We witnessed all of that, which was very exciting to see.

Question 6:

What were your very first thoughts after being raised from the dead?

I was so happy to see Jesus. I was so happy to know that we could go to a special place, that I had been accepted in Paradise, and that they were waiting for Jesus. It truly was paradise, a beautiful place just like heaven is. It had lush trees, and it was so pretty. So I came back from there to life again with a promise that I would see the church grow. I was really happy.

My very first thoughts were happiness at seeing Jesus. I wondered at my memories and at what was happening. "Did I just wake up? I didn't die at all. Was I just sleeping? I am just standing up in this tomb. Why am I here?" But I finally did remember what happened to me, just as people who have near-death experiences remember going to hell or seeing a bright light or going to heaven. Plenty of books have been written about that, and not all of them are Christian. But people have memories and encounters. I certainly remembered Paradise where I had been.

I was very happy to see my sisters because they were heartbroken that I had died. At first, I had to spend a lot of my time consoling my sisters because they were just weeping and weeping aft er I came back. They were now overflowing with joy but overcome with sadness that they had lost me. Now I was back. They were crying tears of sadness and joy. We went back and took off my grave clothes. I had a bath and freshened up, and we ate a delicious meal.

We had certainly created a stir, as I've said. The process of death in the body and the spirit was thought to be finished after three days. The fourth day, it was impossible to be raised, according to Jewish thought. I did something impossible; I came back from the dead after four days. You notice that Jesus resurrected after three days. He didn't do the impossible, at least according to Jewish tradition. His death and resurrection fit into the Jewish understanding.

Jesus didn't appear in public when he came back. He only appeared to believers. He didn't appear in the city for everyone to see. He only appeared to people who'd already believed in him. That's part of the reason that people still doubt that Jesus rose from the dead. He didn't appear in public and make the headlines of the day. They couldn't record that Jesus had been seen in public. He was only seen by his close followers. Jesus chose to do it that way so that we could truly believe in him. Anyone who does believe in Jesus won't be disappointed and let down by him. (See Romans 10:11.)

Question 7:

Why did Jesus weep before he raised you from the dead?

You might be going through a hard time, which might drag on for weeks and weeks. You come across someone who is really close to you, and you just break down in tears and start to cry. That's how Jesus related to my sister, Mary. Martha asked him, "Why weren't you here? If you were here, my brother wouldn't have died." He held his composure, but when Mary came out and asked him the same question, she began to cry, and he cried too.

She was so close to him that she brought out the tears in Jesus. Even though he knew he was going to raise me from the dead, he cried because of her tears. You know how you guys go to movies and the actor is in the middle of an emotional scene and starts to cry, and everyone in the theater starts to cry too. He's just an actor, a fictional movie character, playing a scene. Before he cried in the movie, you didn't even know who he was. Suddenly you are so engaged with the story and involved in the plot so that when he cries, you cry. Mary was very close to Jesus. She pleaded with Jesus, "Why weren't you here? You could have saved him." She started to cry, and Jesus wept too.

He was saddened by the grief of Mary and the others and the actual situation that the Father placed him in. Jesus only did what his Father required of him. As soon as he heard that I was sick, Jesus wanted to come and raise me up with everything that was within him. But it was his Father's will for him to delay until the fourth day and for me to die. Jesus was so submitted to his Father. If Jesus were ever going to disobey his Father, this was when he would have done it. He would have come and prevented my death if he had his way.

If Jesus had lived or responded in the flesh, he would have come and raised me from sickness, and I wouldn't have died. But Jesus was fully submitted to his Father's will. He even delayed coming to see us because his Father told him to wait. I don't know who you are or if you are watching this video or reading this book. A common misconception was that life with Jesus was easy, that living the Christian life is easy. I can tell you the words of Jesus in Luke 9:23, "Then He said to them all, "If anyone desires to come after Me, let him deny himself, and take up his cross daily, and follow Me." Jesus said in Luke 14:26, "If anyone comes to Me and does not hate his father and mother, wife and children, brothers and sisters, yes, and his own life also, he cannot be My disciple."

The Christian life comes with a cost. You can only go up to a certain place into intimacy, the presence of God, and the glory of God, and the power, signs, and wonders of God. You must be willing to pay the price. You can only go to a certain place when you are not obeying him. The Christian life is about obeying the Holy Spirit and being led and ruled by him. When the Holy Spirit or his Father told him to delay in coming to see me, that's what he did. Jesus didn't have it easy: he didn't have an easy life, despite what some people assume. Some people think that he didn't have mockers, that Pharisees weren't crying out for him to be killed, and that people weren't making fun of him, saying, "You think you're the Son of God, well, do this."

Jesus did not have an easy life. From sun up to sun down, people mobbed him and flocked to him to be healed. He never seemed to have a spare minute to himself. That's why our house was so important to him, a place where he could just get away and relax. But he never really relaxed. He was with us, but he was always ministering and busy. He really sowed into people's lives even when he just had time to let his hair down. This was true even as he ate and interacted with others at meals. He would ask you a question before pulling off a piece of bread and chewing it. He gave you time to try and formulate the answer to his question. Like a good rabbi, he asked questions. He asked you a question and pulled off a bit of bread and ate some olives. He ate a couple of olives and a bit of bread, and he waited. You would be waiting for him to speak some more because you don't know the answer to his question. He would just keep eating until you tried to answer his question.

He was amazing, and he pushed you. I think it has come out in interviews before about Peter. He was always the first to try and answer a question. Jesus would ask you a question, and you could see Peter wanted to answer. Jesus would hold up his hand, and say,

"Let Lazarus answer me." And he'd push me like a good friend would push their friends. I wasn't that smart, but I knew his heart. Jesus and I connected heart to heart. He was my friend, and I loved him dearly.

It really made me cry when he was crucified. (Lazarus starts to cry as he mentions this.) Even though I knew what was going to happen, he wasn't recognizable after what they did to him. Isaiah tells us that he was beaten beyond human recognition. "But many were amazed when they saw him. His face was so disfigured he seemed hardly human, and from his appearance, one would scarcely know he was a man" (Isaiah 52:14, NLT). People have no idea what they did to my Savior. His face swelled up so that it was about two feet wide. People like the movie, *The Passion of the Christ*, but even that movie couldn't display what they did to Jesus. People wouldn't sit through a film and watch it if the director, Mel Gibson, had made it any more graphic. They could show it with special effects these days. They can do anything, but people wouldn't be able to sit through a film and watch that happen.

It really broke my heart when he died. I knew he was going to come back from the dead, but what they did to him was beyond words. If people only realized what Jesus willingly went through. If people could only understand what he did for everyone. Who are we? Who are we, as Christians, holding this precious revelation, this precious promise, this precious gift that we have been saved? You, as Christians who have been saved, you look down your nose at other people who aren't saved, who don't know about this wonderful Jesus and what he went through. You look down your nose at people like the Jews who aren't saved.

I used to look down my nose at everyone who wasn't a Jew. The Jews treated Gentiles as a second class of human. The Christian church has sadly done much of the same. They look at Muslims, Buddhists, and Hindus as a lower class of people.

Jesus died for everybody. He died for everybody. He didn't waste his death just for Christians. You need to let people know that Jesus loves them, and you need to be that love to others. When they need a hand out, give them a hand out. When they need a hug, give them a hug and trust the Holy Spirit to bring them into a right relationship with Jesus. Pray for their salvation, and until they ask you questions, just love them. People respond to love. First of all, they want to know what the catch is. When they realize that there's no catch, they want to know what's different about you.

Question 8:

Lazarus, you are one of the few friends that Jesus mentioned in scripture. In fact, scripture says that Jesus loved you. Can you tell us about your friendship with Jesus?

I've covered a lot of that. Jesus was really smart and amazing. He could say the most complex thing, and he could say it so simply. I could understand what he meant. (Lazarus's eyes are full of tears as he mentions this.) He explained the kingdom of God to me. But he didn't explain it in parables. He just explained it. I didn't have to even think. It was just revelation that he gave me. Of course, I was excited when I rose from the dead. I was going to see this kingdom manifest on earth.

I lived to see the Pauls and the Peters and people doing miracles and traveling around our known world at the time. The gospel was setting the world on fire. Jesus was very smart. He was led by the Holy Spirit. Everything he did and said came directly from the throne room. Can you imagine meeting and knowing a person like that, where everything they did came from God? There wasn't one part of flesh in him. He was the kind of person who would finish a conversation before he started a meal or continue a conversation with the person. Instead of dismissing the person, he invited them to come and have a meal with him because it was time for his disciples to eat. He would just invite a leper to our table and think nothing of it. He would tell Mary, "Make a place for him."

He wasn't afraid. He had no fear. In the garden, he had fear because that's where the Spirit of God was starting to leave him. He was shut down. Actually in scripture, he showed his flesh when he was in the Garden of Gethsemane before he died. Even so, he did submit to his Father. You can still actually see him have doubts in this one passage of scripture. But he had no fear or worry. Can you imagine meeting a person who didn't worry or fear? How would your life be, reader? How would your life be if you never struggled with fear or worry again? How would you face the next thirty to forty years that are coming to earth and the coming darkness? How would you face that time if you had no fear and no worry? If you could take fear and worry out of the equation in the Christian life, life would be really sweet, wouldn't it? Well, Jesus never feared or worried until the Garden.

People were always coming to him for money. And he always had enough money to give them. Jesus never turned away anyone for a lack of finances, ever! Ever! He never turned anyone away! He treats people much differently than how the average Christian treats homeless beggars on the street these days. He was very different. He always had enough. He didn't go around asking people for money or charging people to speak. People just flocked to him and gave him money. They gave him sheep, vegetables, food, and blankets. They gave him whatever they could, and he used it. He'd kill a sheep and cook it up as a barbecue and serve a whole lot of people. He taught them all night, and they'd have a roast. He was amazing, and he still is amazing. See, that's the beauty of being a Christian.

You can get to know Jesus. You can talk to him. He can come and visit you in your house. You can interview Jesus and send a video to Matthew. You can tell us all the answers to questions that you've asked Jesus. He's real, but he was amazing. He was a wonderful friend. He used to tell me things that he didn't tell other people. For instance, as I've already told you, he explained the kingdom of God to me, but he didn't use parables. He didn't use complex sayings that were hard to understand. He explained it simply to me because I was a simple person.

When addressing Pharisees, he could quote all the scriptures to back up his arguments. He could enter debates with Pharisees and win every point because every question they asked him was answered by the Holy Spirit with the right scriptures to back up what he said. He could have a tremendously intellectual conversation, words that I heard but did not understand.

Then he could speak to me simply, face-to-face. He explained what went on with the Pharisees and how they were trying to prove he was wrong and how he answered them. He explained it to me in layman's terms as to what just went on, what they were thinking, and how they were trying to trap him, certain traps they had. He was forgiving. A person could slap Jesus in the face, and he would ask him if he needed to slap him again. I've seen him do that. When people were set free from spirits of witchcraft and divination, their masters were not happy. Jesus was slapped. Jesus knew about turning the other cheek because he did it. Some people in the world would slap Jesus. We know at his crucifixion that they pulled and ripped his beard out and spat on him and slapped him. His crucifixion wasn't the first time he was spat on or slapped.

Jesus didn't come to earth to share the impossible, including the gospel, commands and a way of living. Everything he shared was possible. Jesus came with the answer. Search *The Fifty Commands of Jesus Christ* on Google and look it up. You can see what Jesus taught us to do. That's the right way to live. John 14:21 says, "He who has My commandments and keeps them, it is he who loves Me. And he who loves Me will be loved by My Father, and I will love him and [a]manifest Myself to him." If you want to see Jesus, get to know his commands and start to walk in them. You'll see Jesus, and he'll want to meet you. He'll want to show himself to you.

Matthew met him many times in visions. It's so easy for me to sit here with my sisters and speak through Matthew. Matthew has had many hours of conversations with Jesus.

It's very easy for him to sit here, hear me speak, and then speak through me. It takes a lot of faith to do it because of the ridicule and flack that he gets. But it's really easy, and he knows the difference between the Spirit of the Lord and a wrong spirit. It's really easy for him because he's practiced the presence of Jesus and practiced speaking to Jesus. He understands Jesus, so he understands us. All we have to say is that Jesus is amazing. You should get to know him. A lot of you who are watching this video or reading this book don't know him.

What's his favorite television show?

If you took him out to Thai, what curry would he order?

If you took him out to a barbecue, how would he order his barbecue food?

If you took him out for dessert, which dessert would he pick?

Do you know those answers? What's his favorite color? You confessed Jesus; you know Jesus; you go to church every week; what is Jesus's favorite color? Have you ever asked him? Do you know the answer? Do you? (Lazarus chuckles.) Matthew does; he has asked Jesus.

Jesus has things he loves. He loves to talk. The Christian church is out of balance. All they do when they pray is talk, talk, talk. There are 101 books on how to pray but not many books on how to listen. Jesus is really amazing to listen to. You think I'm interesting to listen to? Jesus is even more amazing to listen to. He loves to talk and answer questions. He loves to be pushed. He loves it when you argue with him and say he's wrong. He loves to prove that you are wrong. He doesn't get upset when you argue with him or when you say he's wrong. That proves that you have character and that you just don't accept everything you're told. He loves to be challenged. He loves you to challenge yourself. He loves you. Every word from my mouth is coming from his Holy Spirit. Every word from Matthew's mouth, coming through a word from my mouth, is coming from words that the Holy Spirit has told me to tell you.

Matthew is looking up a scripture right now for me because it fits with what we say. 1 John 2:5–6, "But whoever keeps His [Jesus's] word, truly the love of God is perfected in him. By this we know that we are in Him. He who says he abides in Him ought himself also to walk just as He walked." Do you like that scripture? He who says that he abides in Jesus must walk just like Jesus walks! You didn't even know that was in the Bible. It says that everything you do and say can be led by the Holy Spirit, and you can walk, talk, react, and live just like Jesus lived. Matthew has never heard a preacher preach on that scripture because that would totally blow away our excuses that we're just sinners saved by grace. That would just change the world's perception that you can't be perfect, but you can be, and Jesus is here to help you. He loves you, and I love Jesus. I love him so much. I hope that you have some insight into my friend there. I hope I have sufficiently answered that question for you.

Question 9:

Will you tell us about your two sisters, Mary and Martha, and what they meant to you?

Not a lot is said about Mary and Martha in the Bible. Essentially, we have the story that Mary anointed Jesus's feet and head with oil. (See John 12:3.) And they said of her that if this perfume were sold, it could have brought in a lot of money for the poor. As I've mentioned, we have the famous story of Mary and Martha when Mary sits at the feet of Jesus and Martha is busy in the kitchen. Martha comes out to done. Martha says, "Can't you tell my sister to come and help me?" Jesus lovingly replies to Martha, "Mary's chosen the better thing." (See Luke 10:38–42.)

I will tell you one thing. When you are in the anointing, when the presence of God is thick on you, you lose your appetite. Jesus could speak for twelve hours straight and not have to take a drink or eat. We know this; it's hinted at one time when Jesus was with the Samaritan woman getting some water. He asked for a drink. His disciples come back from town with the food and offered him some. He replied, "I'm already full."

And they said, "Where did you get your food?"

He answered, "I have food that the Father gives me that you don't know of." (See John 4.) That's the anointing. The anointing satisfies you. When Jesus was in the anointing, he didn't have to eat or drink. Anyone who sits under his teaching with the anointing on them doesn't have to eat or drink either. You can be so full of Jesus that you don't have to eat.

Mary was quite happy to wait another three hours until Jesus finished speaking, and she got up and prepared the food. They didn't have to eat. Mary had no compulsion to get up and prepare the food. The spiritual food she was receiving sustained her. People run from conference to conference and book to book and sermon to sermon on YouTube, searching for spiritual nourishment, searching for food. But when the anointing rests on your life, you can pick up the Bible, and one paragraph can blow you away. You might think about that passage for a week or even months. Matthew meditated on the first three verses of Psalm 1 for eight years. Just three verses of scripture for eight years.

Mary loved Jesus. Martha loved him too. But Martha was initially not as connected to Jesus as Mary was. Everyone can learn from the story of Mary and Martha. So many people in ministry start out at the feet of Jesus: soaking, spending time in his presence, reading his Word, meditating, and praying. They spend a lot of time with Jesus. Then revival or a real move of God breaks out in their church. They start receiving invitations to other churches and becoming busy with meetings. They initially started off as a Mary, sitting at Jesus's feet. But then they turn into a Martha, busy with doing ministry. They don't spend time in their secret place with the Lord. Everyone swings between a Mary and a Martha. Marys sometimes wonder if they could do more.

Some people have learned to rest, learned to spend time at the feet of Jesus. But then they worry that they are not doing enough. Some people can't be happy unless they are always busy. And yet there's a happy balance where you can minister out of rest. In that place, you can be very busy but can rest in a blissful state and always spend time with the Lord. For instance, Heidi Baker can spend up to five hours in prayer each morning before she comes out and ministers. She has a very busy ministry of ten thousand churches and ten thousand orphans. Anyone thinks that they could find less time with Jesus, but sometimes she spends up to five hours before she even starts her daily routine.

Jesus was the same with his Father. Often he would stay up all night. Another sign of the anointing is that you don't need sleep. So Jesus could go days at a time and minister all day and stay up with his Father all night. He could go for days like that. Some saints have been recorded to go without sleep for weeks and months. Some saints in history have been recorded to go without food for a year. These things are possible with the supernatural. Mary was a lover, and Martha came around too after Jesus showed her what was best. She relaxed.

I loved Martha. We all need Marthas in our lives. Things just don't get done without someone who is practical. But we all need worship leaders and Marys. We need some pastors that are Marys. We need some prophets that are Marys. We need Marthas to get things done. We need Marys to get things done. We need a combination of both. We need someone who is practical and someone who spends time with the Lord. Jesus was both. Jesus was busy all day and restful at night. But he was even resting while he was ministering. Everything that came to Jesus was orchestrated by the Father and planned by him.

Jesus used to see his whole day of ministry laid out before him as he was in prayer at night. He would see the upcoming day and the miracles. It was no wonder that he healed a certain boy that couldn't be healed by his disciples because he'd seen the boy come to him. He'd heard the conversation from the Father before the Father even presented himself.

You need to be a Mary and a Martha. The Marthas in this world believe a great fallacy that if the world were full of Marys, nothing would get done. People who want to spend time with the Lord and just soak in his presence also sometimes believe a fallacy. A lot of them can be lazy people because they aren't doing anything. God doesn't want you spending all day at his feet without reproducing and bearing fruit.

The Bible calls us to bear fruit. There's a needed balance of both. Mary was a big lover; my sister was a big lover. She really treasured Jesus. Matthew really enjoys doing this interview because he loves to hear me speak. But it's five times better hearing Jesus.

People used to listen all day and all night to Jesus. Paul once preached for eighteen hours straight. Don't you think Jesus would have done it? He was amazing. He is amazing. You should hear him speak.

Mary was a lover. That's why when she cried and said, "Jesus, if you had been here, my brother wouldn't have died," it brought tears to Jesus's eyes. (See John 11:32.) Mary stars in films in heaven. She's a great little actress and a beautiful worshipper. She sings songs in heaven.

Martha is just a delight, and I'm caught because I love both my sisters. Martha was so practical. If you wanted an editor for your book, Martha would be perfect for the job. She just sees everything. She toes the line and is very ordered and structured. She gets things done. If you need a general manager to look after your whole business and run your whole show, you can put Martha in charge. She will get it done. She only had people around her that were movers and shakers.

Mary would be like Benny Hinn's worship leader-speaker, and Martha would be like the general manager that put the show on the road for you. Benny Hinn is a well-known evangelist who goes from stadium to stadium. He needs someone in charge of all the logistics. Martha would be the logistics person. Benny Hinn wouldn't have just anyone as the logistics person. The person would need a very deep relationship with Jesus, and Martha did eventually have that. So I loved both my sisters. It was great to come back from the dead and spend more time with them before I died.

Question 10:

When you died the second time, did you die and get buried, or were you taken up? The scriptures don't tell us this.

Hebrews 9:27 says this: "And as it is appointed for men to die once, but after this the judgment." A lot of people think really holy people don't die; they get taken up. But for that scripture to be true, people have to die. And people who were taken up need to die too, because if they didn't die, that scripture would not be true. People believe that Mary, Jesus's mother didn't die; she ascended. People believe that certain saints like John the disciple didn't die. They have all these assumptions about people who didn't die. How is that scripture? It's appointed once for man to die, then comes a judgement. How would that scripture apply if people didn't die? So I died. That's a quick and easy answer to your question.

Heaven is aware of where this book will go. Heaven is aware of where this interview will go and of what hearts need to be touched. But you certainly need to share this video on Facebook. God bless.

Paul's Comments

This interview has been packed with lots of emotion, moments of laughter and tears expressed by Lazarus. Lazarus opened up his heart for us to connect to him as he shared about his life with Jesus and his siblings, Mary and Martha. This is what I picked up from the interview.

Lazarus's death and resurrection: His death and resurrection served a purpose. Many Jews came to believe in Jesus and follow Jesus because of it. My son passed away a few years ago as a newborn when he was fifteen days old. His sudden death brought much pain, but God poured out so much peace to me and my wife that people were shocked by it. One day, I preached about this, and the altar call was great for salvation, followed by another great altar call for healing for those that had lost their loved ones and their babies. So the death of someone can be an opportunity for people to be saved, healed, or delivered. Every calamity or setback you might experience can serve as a great opportunity for Jesus to use you.

The early church: The early church was a great moment in history. Lazarus emphasized this point: it was great for him to come back and witness the acts of the early church. This point causes us to look at the current church and wonder if it's really living up to the standards of the early church. Are we carrying the baton that the early church has passed on? Or have we lost it somewhere? What baton will we pass to the next generation as a church? Are we walking in the supernatural? Are we walking in signs and wonders? Are we daily walking under an open heaven? Is the world running to the church for answers to today's problems?

A hard life: What came as a shock was how Lazarus described the swollen face of Jesus during the crucifixion. Then he mentioned how Jesus had a hard life, how Jesus was slapped by the masters of those who were sorcerers after Jesus delivered them. Jesus faced many hardships long before the cross. I believe that most of us have no idea what kind of life Jesus lived. Matthew shares more about the life of Jesus in *Jesus Speaking Today* and *Finding Intimacy with Jesus Made Simple*. You will learn about the life of Jesus from his childhood. If you are facing challenges right now, know that Jesus also lived a very hard and difficult life.

Total obedience: Jesus lived a life of obeying the will of the Father. Lazarus mentioned how Jesus walked in the Spirit by obeying the Father instead of following his own will. This highlights the fact that Jesus always mentioned that he did what he saw his Father do. He was in total obedience, regardless of who he was in the Trinity. This calls for us as believers to seek the will of the Father daily and do it. We must seek his perfect will. Lazarus is clear that Jesus could have healed him at his own will, which would have been permissible, but he chose not to. How many of us are choosing the permissible will instead of the perfect will of the Father?

Intimacy with Jesus: The level of friendship that Lazarus had with Jesus was unique. In fact, the three siblings, Mary, Martha and Lazarus, each had a unique friendship with Jesus. Lazarus mentions Mary and Martha extensively in relation to how special they were to Jesus. We learn from this that Jesus wants you to relate to him the way you are and get to know him. Religion has caused people to shy away from asking Jesus questions. They hesitate to address Jesus through their personality and talk to Jesus using the language they are comfortable with. Matthew has written a book called *7 Keys to Intimacy with Jesus*. It will guide you on how to approach Jesus and have a relationship with him.

The heart of a servant: This brings us to a point of servanthood, which is what Jesus said he came for: to serve and not to be served. This speaks to the Marthas and Marys among us. These two sisters were unique, but through wrong interpretation of scripture, we've believed that Martha failed to recognize the importance of sitting at Jesus's feet. Lazarus pointed out that Jesus acknowledged the differences between Mary and Martha. Actually, these two represent how Christians are formed and how we need to strike a balance between the two: a worshipper and a practical person. Both of them have the heart of a servant, and we must not think that one is better than the other. We must see that both the Marys and the Marthas have the Lord's interests at heart.

Find your purpose: As you pursue a relationship with Jesus, one important aspect was that Lazarus, Mary, and Martha had a purpose. What on earth are you here for? This is a very important question and a vital pursuit for all believers. The pursuit of this will lead you to flow in your gifts and learn to know the voice of God. You will be content in your life and not chase after the things of the world and entangle yourself with them. Matthew has written a book called *Finding Your Purpose in Christ*, which can help guide you regarding your purpose in life.

I found the above points important along with other relevant subjects that Lazarus mentioned. I believe that if you read this book more than once, you can find great nuggets. We thank God for using Matthew for this insightful and revelatory interview. God bless.

Interview with Thomas

❖ *Introduction*

This is Matthew Robert Payne, and this is an interview with Thomas, also known in the Bible as Thomas the Doubter. We all remember Thomas in the scriptures for doubting Jesus. I think that we all might have something in common with him. Perhaps you struggle with doubt. I think that this is an issue for everyone. Some people will hesitate to admit that they relate to Thomas, while other people will honestly admit that they deal with doubt.

I have a good friend, Julie. She determines the questions to ask each of the saints. Both of us feel that it is a real honor. It's also nice to have someone else think up the questions. This allows the saint to answer truthfully, rather than just using questions that I might be able to think up the answers for. It allows the saint to speak through me. It certainly keeps me on my toes. Without further ado, I will just start to read the first question from my phone, and we will go from there.

Question 1:

People remember you as doubting Thomas. Jesus walked with you for three years and told you he would return after his death, but you had to see and touch him before you believed. Can you explain why?

First of all, let me say that Jesus rose from the dead, and Mary Magdalene went to report to the disciples that he was risen. They said, "Garbage!" So all the disciples doubted that Jesus rose from the dead, not just me. They actually went to the tomb and found out that he was not there. But they did doubt Mary initially. It is true that Jesus appeared and asked me to put my hand in his side and feel the nail marks in his hands and feet. I did doubt.

I'm not sure how you feel, but doubt is sometimes useful for us individuals. Some people believe blindly. Doubt really is the opposite of faith, so it is true that I doubted, which showed a lack of faith in me. The truth of the matter is that I liked things clear and straightforward. It just seemed too much for me to believe that Jesus had come back from the dead. He did talk about it. But you will recognize that many of the truths that Jesus spoke of in the Bible weren't understood by us disciples until the Holy Spirit had come.

The disciples had been told many times that Jesus would die and rise again on the third day, but none of us understood this. I wasn't the only one. For instance, the disciples on the road to Emmaus were sad, although they were walking with Jesus. They said, "Didn't you hear that Jesus died in Jerusalem? He was the Messiah, and he died." Jesus went on and explained every scripture in the Old Testament about his life, his death, and what was foretold, and they were amazed.

When he went back to break bread with them, they finally realized that it was Jesus, and then he disappeared. So I wasn't the only one who didn't understand that Jesus was going to die and come back. Peter went back to his fishing. The disciples were totally mortified and shocked that Jesus died on the cross and that he was killed. I wasn't the only one surprised by the fact that he died. It was natural and of my flesh that I didn't have the faith to believe that Jesus had risen again.

In some ways, I thought it was just too good to be true. Matthew's brother used to have trouble when his mother went away. One time, she left, and when she came back, he was hiding. He couldn't face his mother. He was too overcome with emotion to come out and greet her when she came back. She found him hiding, and he broke down in tears. In the same way, I was emotional when I heard that Jesus had risen again. It was not only doubt; it was a combination of doubt, fear, and emotion that my Savior had come back.

I am not sure when you are living. It's now been two thousand years since Jesus died. I am not sure if you really realize it, but he was our whole life. We gave up everything and left all to follow him, and then he died out of the blue—at least we thought it was out of the blue. We hadn't heard about his death. We'd heard Jesus say that he would die, but we never understood him. Our spirits didn't hear it. We hadn't really heard of any historical records of people coming back from the dead. Jesus had raised a couple of people from the dead, but we thought those signs were over.

I doubted as part of my natural flesh. I want you to recognize that you doubt Jesus also when he tells you to:

Turn the other cheek. He really means that you should forgive and turn the other cheek instead of being offended again by the same person.

Forgive the person seventy times seven (or 490 times). He really means that you should forgive a person that many times.

Don't take your brother to court. Two Christians fighting in court aren't a good witness to the ungodly judge. He means that you shouldn't go to court about a custody matter or a divorce.

I'm not the only one who doubts Jesus. Jesus said many

things and gave many instructions on how to live the right kind of life. People doubt that his way is better. They doubt him. On one hand, you can say that I doubted that Jesus rose from the dead. At the same time, I can quite clearly say from heaven while watching individuals on earth that they doubt Jesus too. They doubt his words. Jesus said at the end of Matthew 7, after he delivered the Sermon on the Mount, "26 "But everyone who hears these sayings of Mine, and does not do them, will be like a foolish man who built his house on the sand: 27 and the rain descended, the floods came, and the winds blew and beat on that house; and it fell. And great was its fall.""

So many of you understand what Jesus said but ignore it. Many Christians live their lives like that foolish man. Storms haven't attacked you badly enough yet for your whole life to be lost if you don't obey Jesus and follow his commands. Times are coming when those who obey Jesus will survive.

So I just want to address that I'm not the only person who doubted. I doubted, which was a natural human reaction. At least I spoke it out. As I shared, the disciples also doubted when Mary reported that Jesus had risen from the dead.

The Bible records my words in John 20:25, "Unless I see in His hands the print of the nails, and put my finger into the print of the nails, and put my hand into His side, I will not believe." But how many of the seventy that Jesus sent out, how many other believers of Jesus, actually doubted too? I was the only one recorded who verbalized my doubts. Sometimes many people in the crowd are actually thinking something, and then someone speaks up and asks the question. Well, the person who asks the question says what ten others were thinking, but the one who asks the question has the attention of the speaker. The other nine people have their question answered, but they just didn't speak up.

I put this idea to you. Was I the only one doubting? Or was I just the one who spoke my thoughts out loud? Are you doubting Jesus? If you're not, why aren't you doing everything he told you to do?

Question 2:

Jews attempted to stone Jesus in Judea, and when the disciples didn't want to go there, you said, "Let us also go, that we may die with him." (See John 11:16.) Can you explain what was in your heart that day?

I was passionate for Jesus. He was my life. This was part of why I doubted. He was so much a part of my life that I couldn't believe he was back. Jesus was my everything. To live with him, to die with him was an honor. According to history, I wasn't the only Christian who died for my faith. The early Christians were fed to the lions and went out singing joyfully. Many Christians were recorded as singing on their way to their execution and went to face death with joy.

There's a joy, a certain intimacy, a certain love that you can have for Jesus that brings you into a sense of abandonment, and you totally forsake your flesh. You let go of your flesh, and everything is given over to your relationship with Jesus. Have you reached that place yet? Have you reached the point where you come to the end of yourself and a beginning with Jesus? Have you reached a place where you can't find the defining line between you and Jesus?

I can tell you that as disciples, we lived and breathed Jesus. We listened to him talk for fifteen hours straight sometimes. His words, like Mary said, were as intoxicating as alcohol is intoxicating to a person. He was addictive to listen to. He was amazing, just amazing. You can't define him. He was out of this world—totally, totally shocking. He was completely different, and that's what he called us to be. I was willing to do anything with Jesus. I was quite willing to go to the city and be stoned with him. I was totally committed to him. Julie, I hope that I have explained that answer for you.

Question 3:

Did you have a twin, and if so, can you tell us about him?

I didn't have a twin, yet I have many brothers in Christ. Some of the disciples became close and bonded with each other. When I left for

India, I took a couple of people to serve with me that were very close to me. I had an intimate relationship with these people. Not everyone in the Bible, not everyone who served Jesus, receives recognition, but people who served with me were very precious to me. This is just like people today who serve with a pastor or with someone in ministry or your Christian brother or sister who has seen you cry and been through the valleys with you and supported you. Those people become very precious to you.

Question 4:

Did you witness the Assumption of Mary into heaven? What was it like?

Mary, Jesus's mother, addressed this question in her interviews in *Great Cloud of Witnesses Speak*, saying that she died a natural death. I did not witness her assumption into heaven. The Bible records for people to read, "And as it is appointed for men to die once, but after this the judgment" (Hebrews 9:27). The two people recorded in the Bible who didn't die are Enoch and Elijah. They are due to come back to the earth and serve as two witnesses and be killed on the streets. At that time, they will die too.

Part of the curse, part of the judgement of God, is that everyone dies. As much as it's a nicely held belief, there really isn't much difference between someone dying of old age when their spirit leaves them or their whole body going to heaven. Mary was a saint and a beautiful person. She had a peaceful death. She has spent the rest of her time in a glorious position in heaven. She's known in heaven as the mother of Jesus. She's highly revered in heaven, and she spends a lot of her time there with a prayer shawl, interceding for the saints on earth, for certain people in the world.

She actually does hear the prayers of the saints on earth. She adds her prayers to their prayers and presents them to Jesus and the Father. Many Protestants might have an issue with this, but God is a big God. As long as people are praying, he's happy. God is happy with the people who highly revere Mary. But some people think they could be committing idolatry by worshipping her. They are not aware of how God feels. You are really innocent when you have a childlike faith and when you believe certain things that you've been taught.

Like I said, Mary spends a lot of her time interceding for people on earth. She's highly revered in heaven. She's taken a lower position in heaven, similar to Jesus's words when he said in Matthew 20:26b, "But whoever desires to become great among you, let him be your servant." Mary is really humble and busy and a servant to all. She's a great mother figure to have in heaven. She doesn't have a lot of time on her hands when she's not doing anything. She really is focused with serving others. She has a real heart for others. I hope that answers your question.

Question 5:

It is said that while you were in India, you transported to Mary's tomb. Is that true?

Matthew has no idea whether this is true, but I'm answering this question, and I am here. It is true that it happened. I had such great faith and great love for Mary that the Lord allowed me to translate. Many saints and mystics in the Bible and since then have translated. God knew that it was important to me, so it happened. Matthew has no further knowledge of anything about this subject, but I can just confirm that those reports are true. I hope that encourages you, Julie. I hope it encourages the people who believe it happened. Matthew is happy that one of the questions was answered in what he assumes is the right way.

Question 6:

Around 52 A.D., you went to India to spread the Christian faith. Can you give us any wisdom today about how to witness to the same types of people?

The Indian Hindu religion has millions of gods with real entities, demons, behind these gods. The demons can do signs and wonders. Matthew has heard of a man who used to walk along the street and levitate a towel above his head to keep him in the shade. He didn't have an umbrella. He just took a towel out and made the towel levitate above his head.

That seems natural to a spiritual person in India. My advice, the wisdom I can give to you, is when you want to minister in a country that recognizes spiritual activity, use your God-given authority and power. Release the power of God to the blind people: let them receive sight. To the deaf people: let them be able to hear. To the crippled: raise them up. The Indian people respect the power of God. Learn and seek out the people that are walking in power and go and emulate their lives.

They also respond like anyone else to agape, the unconditional love of Jesus Christ. You can quite possibly break through to a hardened person simply by listening to them and spending time with them. Over the course of the week, you might spend ten hours listening to a person unburden themselves to you. You never waste time when you listen to people. Some people hurt so deeply that they just need to talk and talk and talk. Sometimes you need to have the patience and the grace of Jesus to be able to breakthrough to these people. Some people finally run out of things to say when they know that you will listen because no one has ever really listened to them before. Then their doors are open, and their defenses are down, and they are willing to hear the message of Christ.

Too many people think that angry preaching about Jesus

Christ is the answer. Too many people walk around saying repent or burn. Too many people force Jesus down another person's throat without giving them two dollars to buy food. We need to come with an answer. If people are blind, we need to open their blind eyes. If people are deaf, we need to open their deaf ears. If people believe a certain idea that gives confidence and understanding, we need to bring a better idea that gives them more confidence and more understanding.

There isn't a set answer, but I learned the power of Jesus. I carried the power of the Holy Spirit and took that to India with the love and compassion of Jesus. I learned to be in Jesus and for Jesus to be in me. I carried the presence of Jesus everywhere I went, and I shone with the glory of Jesus, and the people knew there was something different about me. That's the wisdom of God, which will still work with the tribes of Africa and the Indian people today. You take the miraculous power of God and release it into the villages of India. It will still work today with the people. So many people are bound up with demonic oppression and diseases from the enemy. All you need to do is go in there with power and set people free.

Question 7:

It is said that you fought darkness and the master of darkness himself in India. It is said that you made Satan cry. What wisdom can

you impart to us so that we can do the same?

I think the best thing you can do is understand who you are. I think that the vast majority of Christians have no understanding of their oneness with Christ. They don't understand the power of the Godhead that raised Jesus from the dead that resides in them. They don't understand that just as Christ lives, so can they. They don't understand that Jesus has power that's available through the Holy Spirit to every believer.

I think that's the well-kept secret; it's not taught correctly in churches, books, seminars, and in conferences. They say that that you need to go and get an impartation from Benny Hinn or from this or that big-name speaker to release the glory of God into you. The Holy Spirit is pretty powerful. He just needs you to get a little bit of your flesh outside of yourself so that you can allow the Holy Spirit to possess you, because the Holy Spirit can do great things.

Jesus was my entire being, and I made Satan cry because I came out victorious. I was once a man who doubted, but I overcame doubt and became fully possessed with Jesus, with mighty power and mighty authority. How many people would travel from Jerusalem to India by foot for the sake of the gospel? How many people would travel that far to spread the gospel? That's a pretty long and awesome missionary journey. Of course, an enemy was in that land. Of course, there was opposition. But I came with power, and I represented Jesus, and I'd met and walked and talked with Jesus. When the Holy Spirit came, I felt him in me. I felt him, and I became one with Jesus.

I spent many times—many times—in communion, in prayer, and talking with Jesus face-to-face. Jesus and I walked the roads of India together. He would show me visions of what I was going to do, and I would do it later that afternoon. I walked under an open heaven. I visited heaven all the time. I saw what I was to do, and then I did it. I walked just like Jesus did, which made the enemy sad. If more people would just realize this, if they could just comprehend how powerful they could be, the world would be shaken.

The enemy really has the Christian church bound up with lies. You really can be one with Christ. You really can be possessed by the Holy Spirit. You really can go out and change your nation. You really can. You really can make a video on YouTube that goes viral and affects twenty million people. You really can do things like that. You can get in touch with the president of a country whose daughter is dying of cancer, and you can lay hands on her and heal her. And then the president can recommend you to all the states and all the governors with sick children, family members, and friends.

You might gain a reputation overnight as a healer simply by possessing and confessing Jesus. I only bring one thing to you today and that's Jesus Christ, the fullness of him dwelling in you in a bodily form. If people could only capture:

That you can be a little Jesus in this world.

That you can make a difference. It really isn't you vs. the world; it's Jesus vs. the world. It's Jesus in you and through you, and alive in you today. If people could only get a hold of that.

That they need to die to themselves and let go of the passions of the flesh.

That they should only enter the narrow road and live a life that is free from the bondages of the flesh.

That the flesh can be overcome and that Jesus Christ through his Holy Spirit can reign in them.

That they can be possessed by the Holy Spirit and walk with him.

That Jesus can dominate them.

So many people believe that you can be possessed by demons, which is true; you can be. If someone has a controlling or a Jezebel spirit, everything they do might be controlling and wicked. Their whole lives can be dominated by that spirit. Well, that's easy. Christians believe that it's true. People can have a Jezebel spirit that smears and colors everything that they do. Why can't the same Christians believe that you can be possessed by Jesus? You can then do everything that he does. And everything you do looks like Jesus and sounds like him. Why can't people believe that? They can believe that a demon can do it, but they can't believe that Jesus can actually possess you and control your body. Well, he can!

Jesus said, "Unless a grain of wheat falls into the ground and dies, it remains alone; but if it dies, it produces much grain." (See John 12:24.) Jesus said, "For whoever desires to save his life will lose it, but whoever loses his life for My sake will find it." (See Matthew 16:25.) Jesus spoke a lot about death and rebirth. You can die to self; you can have a crucifixion. We were all co-crucified with Christ. Behold, a new person lives in you. It's just a lie that propagates that you're still alive. You were co-crucified with Christ at your conversion. You can live this new life. This new life made me a powerhouse in India.

Question 8:

Many ideas abound on how you died: a hunter shooting a peacock accidentally shot you with two arrows, stoned and lanced by a local priest, martyred in East Persia with four spears by local soldiers, and a natural death in Edessa. Can you enlighten us?

The truth is that I was stoned and lanced by a local priest. The other stories are just religion. Religion can be really bad, you know. Some people can jump into faith and have a whole lot of rules and live their lives as if they are wearing blinders. Anyone that doesn't conform to their rules is a heretic or speaking heresy and should be dealt with severely. The Holy Spirit doesn't fit into rules very well. The Holy Spirit is free. For example, interviews with saints, saints coming down from heaven to visit Matthew and answer questions through Matthew, and these types of matters are way out there on the fringe.

Religious people would want to shut this down and stop it. If this were broadcast on international TV, thousands of Christians globally would make an outcry saying, "Take that off TV. That's heresy. It's false and not right. He's a false prophet." Religious people, people with religion, will always act out.

People with authority, with advertising rights on the TV station, would pull their advertising, saying, "Take that off, or I will pull my advertising." They would threaten to remove the show, and sometimes religious people might kill the move of God. Religious people killed Jesus, and I was killed by religion as well. But like I said before, I was willing to die with Jesus, and it was an honor for me. Once you are completely committed to Jesus, death isn't scary.

Question 9:

Thomas, I understand that you were a very experienced carpenter. Did you design or

build any of the churches in India?

I assisted with a couple of churches being built by builders, and I put in a lot of time. Sometimes we'd go to a certain place, and I needed a church there. I would assist the local builders and contribute my labor for free. The people fed me and looked after me. We used their material. Just like today, it's no different when a carpenter in a Christian church can help build churches or work on other projects around the church. If he were on a mission field, he'd be building churches. So that's not a big deal. It was just part of my ministry.

I also raised over a hundred people from the dead. That's a more impressive feat. Raising people from the dead in India certainly impresses the Hindus. They don't have that type of power, so it certainly causes many revivals wherever you do that.

I was always involved in more than looking for places to build churches. I could actually build a church community through one prayer for a person and raising a person from the dead. I could start a whole church of new converts from one miracle. You take that one to the bank, more than one hundred people raised from the dead, although I won't say the exact number. But more than one hundred people were raised from the dead through my ministry. Along the way, I had help and expertise from the local people in building certain churches.

I really loved helping in any way I could. I served food. I bandaged wounds. I healed deaf people and blind eyes. I raised people from the dead. I was poisoned once, but the poison didn't work. I had many attempts on my life before I was actually killed. I survived a lot of them until God chose the time for me to die.

Question 10:

What's the greatest treasure, teaching, or revelation that you received from Jesus while he walked this earth?

I think I previously covered that when I was talking about overcoming Satan. It's possible for us to be possessed by Jesus and to be one with him and to walk in the full demonstration of his power and do greater works than Jesus. It's possible to be one with Jesus and to be in Christ. I certainly learned a lot from Jesus, and I learned a tremendous amount from the Holy Spirit. Surprisingly Mary Magdalene and I spent a lot of time together. She was mystical, a very deep thinker.

Actually, the rumor should not be about her relationship with Jesus but about her relationship with me because we spent so much time together. She's a beautiful person. She's very deep and very mystical. I learned oneness with Christ, how to walk in that oneness, and how to be possessed by Jesus through Mary's example.

You would do well to listen to what she has to say in her interviews. You would do well to read what Matthew brings from her because she has a tremendous relationship with Jesus Christ. I think I covered it for you. It's possible to be one with Jesus and to be fully possessed by him. John 15 covers that when Jesus says, "I am the vine, and you are the branches." The same chapter also talks about abiding, and to abide in Jesus, you need to obey him. All of these truths are connected. You can't abide in Jesus unless you die to self. When you die to self and start to live according to Jesus, you will follow Galatians 5:16. "I say then: Walk in the Spirit, and you shall not fulfil the lust of the flesh." Dying to self, walking in the Holy Spirit, and obeying the commands of Jesus allows you to abide in him. When you abide in him, there's nothing you can't do and no prayer that won't be answered.

You put Jesus first. I'll confess that Jesus is Lord of my life. He's still the Lord of my life, and I pray that he'd be Lord of your life. God bless you and keep you, and may the Father shine his light upon you. As you listen to this and enjoy it, may the favor of God start to manifest in your life. Amen. God bless. Bye-bye.

Paul's Comments

This was one of the great interviews that Matthew did. Thomas spoke through Matthew, and Julie submitted the questions. Julie asked interesting questions that everybody would have wanted to know from Thomas, particularly the question about Thomas doubting Jesus. I think that question stood out among others. I am also guilty of wondering how Thomas could have doubted Jesus.

When we read the Bible, we sometimes think we know the answers. I believe that's because we already know the end of the story or what's to come. It's like watching TV with a show with dramatic irony. You know who the bad guy is while the police are searching without a clue or a hope of catching the bad guy. They finally find one simple thing that leads them to the bad guy. We wonder how they missed it all along, and we think that they were foolish. Well, that's how we read most of the stories in the Bible—from hindsight—and we have our own opinions about the characters.

We wonder why Adam bit the fruit too. We wonder how David could do what he did with Bathsheba and how he could kill her husband. We wonder how Peter could deny Jesus three times after he had been warned about it. We think that we wouldn't do that if we were them. We think we know better. Well, that's a lie that Satan catches us in for years. We think we know because we have also relied on others to interpret the Bible for us instead of asking the Holy Spirit to bring a revelation of what's written in the Bible. We are called to have a relationship with Jesus, a relationship with the Holy Spirit and with the Father. When we neglect these, we are bound to fall into deception and religion. We can greatly miss out because of this neglect.

We should listen to others preach or teach, but we must come to a point of searching the scriptures ourselves and finding revelation from the Holy Spirit. If we don't do that, we will end up caught up in a lie like the one that the Apostle Thomas exposed, whereby Christians think that we must receive power from someone else to do mighty works, not knowing that the Holy Spirit in us is all powerful to use us. This was a revelation to me because I believed that lie before I heard this message.

What additional lies have we been caught up in as believers? What I love about this interview is that it also highlights other truths in Matthew's books that we were not aware of.

The Apostle Thomas suggested that you check out what Matthew has written about Mary Magdalene. You can find her interviews in *Mary Magdalene Speaks from Heaven: A Divine Revelation* and *Mary Magdalene Speaks from Heaven, Book 2: A Divine Revelation*. One of the questions also asked about Mary, the mother of Jesus. Please read her interview in *Great Cloud of Witnesses Speak.*

Apostle Thomas also mentioned that Christians need to know who they are in Christ to do great works. Check out *Your Identity in Christ* and *Influencing Your World for Christ* to learn more about how you can practically impact this world every day. I like how he mentioned that you can win somebody to Christ by simply listening to them and spending time with them. We can all do that. Lastly, check out Matthew's book, *Walking under an Open Heaven*. Thomas mentioned that he walked with Jesus daily under an open heaven so that he went to heaven while still here on earth.

The more closely we walk with Jesus and obey his commands, the more closely we bring heaven to earth, the more his kingdom comes, and the more we rule and reign as Christians in this world. I hope that this interview was a great blessing to you. We thank God for using Matthew to bring about such an interview for all that seek to know him and do his will. God bless.

Interview with Timothy

❖ *Introduction*

Hello, this is Matthew Robert Payne, and this will be an interview with Timothy from the Bible, the young man who traveled with Paul on extensive missionary journeys and who was mentored by Paul. We are just going to go ahead with some of the questions that I have been given by a friend.

Julie has developed the questions for the saints. I enjoy getting questions that I hadn't thought of before. I can't make up these questions for the interview myself, which is excellent. I hear answers that I can't make up. We welcome Timothy here today. He's welcomed, and we'll go ahead with the questions.

Question 1:

Timothy, we know from scripture that Eunice, your mother, and Lois, your grandmother, were Jewish and were believers and taught you scriptures while you were very young.

a) What influenced you most to learn about the faith when you were so young?

I have to say that some people are naturally attracted to the things of God. Certain young individuals are passionate about Jesus from an early age. I was one of those children. I was certainly interested in God and in everything of God. My parents, my mom, and my grandmother influenced me in that way. I was like a dying person in a desert who comes across an oasis. They go to the oasis; they drink their fill and eat as much fruit and food found at the oasis as possible. I was sort of like a starving child.

We have to remember that God ordains certain people to live on the earth. God ordains their destiny and their purpose. I was created to be mentored by Paul and then go on and be a teacher of the Christian faith and evangelist and share my faith with non-believers. My destiny was to become a bright light for Jesus in the communities where I lived. It was only right and destined for me to spend so much time learning about the scriptures, about God, about my traditions as a partially Jewish boy and the understanding of my mother's and my grandmother's beliefs.

This wasn't strange to me. It wasn't as though I was being force-fed information. As I described, I was like a starving man in a desert. The scriptures of God, the information about God, and what my grandmother and my mother showed me were like an oasis to me.

b) Were you influenced much by your Greek Gentile father?

I loved my father. Every man receives his self-esteem from his father. I was no different. My father was a very gentle man, a gentleman. He influenced my life through his love and acceptance. He was married to my mother, who was a Jew, and he fully supported her teaching me the Jewish faith. He was very welcoming and open to my studies. He was fairly influential in the town where we lived. He was successful in business, and I loved him very much. He was important to me.

He liked my mother's faith, and you could say that he secretly believed in the Jewish God too. You certainly don't have mixed marriages unless one partner has really come to grips with the other partner's faith. Mixed marriages don't seem to work culturally without a bit of give and take. My father certainly demonstrated a lot of give. He approved it when I went away with Paul and encouraged me in all I did and said.

c) How did this mixed marriage affect you?

I wouldn't necessarily use the word affect to describe what happened. For instance, Australia has different cultures for Matthew to experience. The Chinese congregate in certain suburbs and make Chinese food. They influence the culture and add flavor. The mixed marriage in my life just added flavor and context to what I believed. I understood my father's traditions and beliefs that he held before he was married to my mom. He is in heaven now, and he was converted to the Christian faith.

My father was very open. It wasn't that my mother was domineering or pushy about her faith. She believed it and was passionate about it, which influenced my father. Both my mother and my grandmother came to the Christian faith when the Christian faith was preached to them, but they had a very strong foundation in their Jewish faith. I had a great upbringing with a lot of flavor, a lot of contextual flavor through the different beliefs and the backgrounds of my parents.

I really admired the strong Jewish tradition in my family. It helped me understand Paul because he was a strong Jew. When I met him, he always had a strong residue of the Jewish faith in him. He never departed from the understanding of the Jewish poetic books, the prophets, and the Torah. He never departed from it. He just worked out his salvation and his faith according to the Christian belief, according to what Christ taught. He worked it around the Jewish faith, but he eliminated the portions that weren't to be obeyed anymore, and he continued with the new covenant.

Question 2:

How did you have the courage to leave your family to go with Paul at such a young age?

Paul had a reputation as someone who was highly learned with a lot of teaching and knowledge. He carried himself very well. He was all business. He was passionate for Jesus. He had a laid-down crucified life for Jesus. He showed that he was professional in the way he dressed and spoke. But he had this passion, this attractive zeal.

As a young boy, I was attracted to him. I was blessed that he wanted to mentor me and that he wanted me to come with him. My parents were overjoyed at the fact that I was chosen to be trained up in the new Christian faith. They were very supportive, but if they hadn't been supportive, I wouldn't have gone with him because I had tremendous respect for them. They met Paul, and Paul encouraged them and pled his case for why he wanted to take me under his wing. They were overjoyed.

You have to remember that in those days, being a rabbi or a spiritual leader was very important. Today, it's not as important to be seen as a preacher or a pastor. They certainly respect the position in your modern day, but when I lived, it was a lot rarer and was a more privileged position. It was like a judge in your modern society: highly revered and highly respected and not everyone could follow that path. I was very excited and easily convinced to become Paul's student. I hope I covered that correctly.

Question 3:

What made you so passionate for the knowledge of Jesus Christ and living as a disciple under Paul to learn more about Jesus?

As I said, I grew up in the Jewish faith with a thirst like a man in the desert searching for water. It was birthed in my DNA. My character was carved by God. My destiny was established to be part of the Christian faith, and God ordained for me to be converted and to be convinced of the Christian faith. He had my destiny all planned out to follow Paul and to be part of that. It really came naturally to me. It was just a natural progression of what I learned from my mother and my grandmother. It was exciting news.

I also had a visitation from Jesus in a dream, and he called me forth and commissioned me to serve with Paul. I shared this with Paul, and he told me that was a confirmation of his own understanding and his own leading to take me on. It actually reinforced Paul's commitment as he knew that Jesus had endorsed me as his follower. Although that's not in the scriptures, Jesus commonly appeared to believers in dreams and visions. Later as I traveled with Paul, I also experienced seeing Jesus in visions.

Seeing Jesus in visions should be a natural part of the Christian life. It's part of your inheritance and available to most Christians if they have the faith, the childlike faith, to accept that it is possible. Global schools of the supernatural are starting to emerge that are teaching and sharing this and encouraging people to have visions. Matthew can certainly encourage you to experience this and to press into this because meeting Jesus face-to-face is exciting. It's always wonderful to talk to Jesus.

Just as I am here speaking through Matthew, visions are part of what he does. He can see me through a vision. He can hear my words coming directly into his heart. This is all supernatural. So I saw Jesus in a dream, and he instructed me to go with Paul and be a part of Paul's mission. Of course, like I said, that's not in the Bible.

The scriptures tell us that if everything Jesus did during his life were documented, there wouldn't be enough books to contain it all. There wouldn't be enough room in the world for the books that would describe what Jesus said and did. (See John 21:25.)

Many things happened to us saints that weren't in the Bible. We are not adding to the Bible by sharing this. The Bible is complete and a revered part of the Christian faith. It stands alone without needing proof. It's wonderful to know that you can have true experiences like the saints did even though these aren't recorded in the Bible.

Question 4:

How would you describe the changes, if any, between Paul's first visit to Ephesus and his second visit when you left to go with him around 52 A.D?

It was different because I was there and was part of the ministry. Paul gave me opportunities to share my testimonies, to share my faith. Prominent in those testimonies was the dream and the visions I had of Jesus, and I encouraged people to walk in the supernatural and to know Jesus the same way. I had a strong understanding of the Jewish faith, of God, his law, and his holy commands.

From time to time, I spoke as Paul allowed me to speak and share with the people. It was not so much a master-servant sort of relationship, just like Jesus with his disciples. He sent out his disciples to heal the sick and announce that the kingdom had come. So too with Paul. He didn't just teach me and take me under his wing, but he gave me practical experience and things to do. And certainly on that second visit, I was encouraged to play a part, which I did.

In all the places that Paul and I went together, he arranged certain opportunities for me to speak and share. A lot can be done over a dinner table, sharing face-to-face with people, talking and sharing your faith. I was at every dinner table Paul was at. I was invited to the rich people's houses to meet important dignitaries and important people in cities where we went. I was part of the conversation at the dinner table. So I influenced those I came in contact with.

The Holy Spirit can speak through any willing vessel. I was certainly a passionate and willing vessel. From time to time, Paul understood that the Holy Spirit had a message that he put on my heart. He'd let Paul know, and Paul would ask me to speak what the Lord had put on my heart. He knew that under the influence of the Holy Spirit, I could be as well-spoken as he was because the Holy Spirit doesn't change. The influence is the same through anyone's mouth. So Paul shared his platform with me. I learned a lot from speaking and from my mistakes. Paul mentored me in a practical way that was full of experience. I was overjoyed and loved the process.

Question 5:

Paul spent more time with you than with anyone else. What two or three insights about Paul would you want us to know?

First of all, I want to make it clear that Paul was one of the most, if not the most, passionate person in the Christian faith. He was not afraid of conflict or even of death. He was not afraid of people or of being hurt. He possessed no fear and had such passion, such a fire of the Holy Spirit burning within him. Today if Paul were alive, he'd be a big deal. He'd be tearing up revivals and doing a great work in the world. He wouldn't back down from speaking the truth. For instance, if your prime minister in Australia was in an adulterous relationship or a lesbian like some political leaders, he'd certainly speak out about it if given the opportunity or if asked what he thought about a lesbian running the country. He'd certainly say that it's not the best way to live.

In the same way, if a prime minister were in a relationship outside of marriage, like one of your past prime ministers, he'd speak about that. He would say that marriage is a godly covenant, whether or not the individuals are believers. They should be married if they are going to have sexual relations. He was very straight and to the point. He was passionate and fearless. That's a rare quality among people today. People today are full of fear, fear about many things. The Apostle Paul was not afraid of anything or anyone. He was fierce and on fire with the Holy Spirit. He was fearless and passionate.

I've seen him preach for fifteen hours and more. The Bible recorded that he once preached from noon to midnight, and a man fell from the roof. He raised the man from the dead and then preached for another six hours. (See Acts 20:7–12.) Paul was addictive. Listening to him was amazing. The knowledge, the insight, and the revelation of the Holy Spirit that came through Paul was simply amazing. He was breathtaking to listen to. The fact that he had enough resources and enough to say for eighteen straight hours was an amazing feat. Many preachers today will prepare for ten to twenty hours to preach a one-hour sermon. Paul's life was preparation, and he lived a life of revelation.

He was always being caught up to the third heaven, and he spent a lot of time in visions with Jesus. He had a very close relationship with the Holy Spirit who led all his actions. Acts mentions that he made decisions about visiting certain places because of the Holy Spirit. The Holy Spirit restrained him from going to certain places. (See Acts 16:6–7.) He was controlled by the Holy Spirit. The Holy Spirit, not the flesh or sin, reigned in his life.

Paul was a perfected Christian who lived a holy life. He was ruled by the Holy Spirit. He was as good and as effective as Jesus Christ. (See Galatians 2:20.) He did many signs and wonders. He spoke and acted with a demonstration of the Holy Ghost, a demonstration of power, signs, and wonders. He didn't preach any empty gospel or speak about a Jesus that wasn't real. The Jesus that he spoke about manifested in the meetings, and people were healed and set free. (See Acts 14:8–10.) He didn't just say one thing and do another. He wasn't hypocritical. He was so passionate that you just had to be caught up with him in his faith.

He was very encouraging and persuasive in his arguments, illuminating and full of revelation in what he said. He spoke many times about new things. He received fresh revelation as he spoke. The Holy Spirit supplied him with the words, which amazed him. We would talk after he'd spoken, and he would be amazed as he recounted some of the points that the Holy Spirit had made. He wanted to remember those insights to share again in the future.

He was full of insight, full of knowledge. He was certainly to be revered by the saints of God, which you can tell from reading the books that he's written in the Bible. He certainly should be respected beyond what people do today. He was and is tremendous. He teaches and instructs people in heaven. There are so many levels to the glory of God and so many practical steps people can take. He takes people from glory to glory in heaven and from one level of understanding to another level.

He's just on fire for God and is a vessel that the Holy Spirit clearly speaks through. He has an amazing intellect and intelligence. He can process really complex thoughts. He took the Old Testament and spent time with Jesus and came up with the teaching of the new covenant through his epistles and teachings. He's a tremendous reader and learner. He sits under powerful teaching himself and recycles the very best of what he hears. He sits under the prophets of the Old Testament as they speak in heaven about their books and about their lives. He sits under their teaching and then takes that and refocuses it, remodels it, and shares it with the people.

He's a great encourager. You will all want to meet him when you get to heaven and will certainly want to sign up for his classes. He has all different grades of classes in heaven: beginner, intermediate, and advanced. Paul has a lesson for you no matter:

- Where your walk is on earth
- Where you are spiritually
- How much you process on earth
- How dynamic your relationship is with God, or
- How experienced you are in the things of God.

If you are experienced and if you know a lot about Jesus with a lot of great revelations and tremendous insight into spiritual matters, the Apostle Paul can teach you more and give you greater depth and take you further into those insights. He can take anyone further, and he's an amazing teacher. He can teach a baby, and he can teach a fully-grown adult. He has a wonderful gift for teaching and a patience and love that comes with being an excellent teacher.

Paul didn't have favorites. He treated everyone equally with fervent love for each one. But in saying that, he's just like God. People were gifted and passionate, and he spent more time with the gifted and the passionate ones and sowed more into them because they wanted to know more, and they were hungry for more. He filled me up, and I have to say that I am very encouraged to be here today and to be able to speak about him and share with you that Paul was the best thing since sliced bread. He deserves the honor and respect of all Christians. He has gone on and continues to serve God in heaven, teaching people and changing lives and taking people from glory to glory in heaven.

Question 6:

Timothy, I'm sorry that I'm mentioning Paul so much, but we learned about you through Paul and his ministry.

a) You coauthored so many of the epistles with Paul. Can you tell us about that?

I did help Paul with organization and with some of his thoughts in his epistles. Paul was an extraordinary individual and could have written all of it on his own. The only reason that some people say that I coauthored part of what he wrote is because he asked me for insight and for my input into some of what he was saying. We discussed what his message would be and what he would say to people. We discussed what my thoughts were.

Sometimes he incorporated my thoughts on the discussion into what he wrote. I am hesitant to say that I coauthored the books, but I certainly provided input. Most of the books are flavored with Paul, with his love, his language, and his insight. I did influence some of what he wrote, but I hesitate to say that I coauthored the books. I'd just say that it's just as the Holy Spirit influences your life and what you say. People generally recognize you as the author of the book if you write a book. Matthew does recognize the Holy Spirit as the coauthor in what he says because the Holy Spirit is the biggest influence on him.

I wasn't a major influence in what Paul was writing as Paul was mostly influenced by the Holy Spirit in everything he said and did. He just considered what I said in discussions when he wrote to the people. If we had the scriptures opened up, I could point to certain sentences and what he said that I influenced, but we don't have the time. And perhaps if you want to see me in heaven and sit down with me to discuss some scriptures, I could show you those things if you are interested. It's like being mentioned in the acknowledgments of a book when you played a significant role in the book. I would just be happy to be named in the acknowledgments.

b) What was it like to be mentored by Paul?

Paul was very patient and very understanding. As I've said at length, Paul was a passionate man full of zeal. He was a holy man; he didn't go around sinning. He was a tremendous teacher with an extraordinary gift. He has so much compassion, love, and patience that he'd teach you the same thing three times, but you wouldn't notice him becoming frustrated, repeating himself three times to a person who was hard of hearing or hard of understanding.

He was very understanding, compassionate, and full of love. He was an amazing person to be mentored by. I am very humbled to say that I was taught and instructed by Paul. I was certainly very encouraged when he wrote the books of 1 and 2 Timothy to me and gave me further instruction. That's just an example; those books are an example of the way Paul spoke to me and shared things with me. He was so encouraging to me. I had my faults, insecurities, and my fears. He was able to make me bold and courageous. He filled me up so much with scripture, faith, and revelation that I became very bold and courageous for the faith. That was a little bit about Paul as a mentor.

c) How was he as a teacher?

I have covered that in the last question, and I have explained how Paul was as a teacher. I hope that you understood my point. I wish that Paul could write books on grace, leadership, the apostolic, or the prophetic. I wish that heaven would allow Paul to dictate how-to-books to the current generation. They'd certainly be surprised at his knowledge, revelation, and insight. They'd be surprised at the way that he wrote things that were simple and easy for this current generation to understand. He's an extraordinary teacher.

He's one of the best teachers that you'll ever come across. I've sat under many of the teachers in heaven, and Paul is just a light. He shines as a bright light in heaven. He shone as a bright light on earth. He was very encouraging, so very encouraging. You want that quality of encouragement in a teacher. He constantly tested me and my knowledge to reinforce what I'd understood and what I had captured. I did really well with him. His method, his understanding, his love, and compassion made him such a great teacher.

Question 7:

1 Corinthians 16:10 mentions that you were reserved or timid. Would you say that's true, or was that Paul's perspective? How do you see it?

I was sort of timid and reserved, but through Paul's influence, revelation, and the practical demonstration of his life, I became more bold and courageous. I did develop and mature. I did become a little bit bolder and more courageous, but at first, I certainly was timid and reserved as Paul said. That was just my character and who I was, but I became a better person through the indwelling of the Holy Spirit, the teaching of Paul, the revelations that God gave through Paul, and a deeper understanding of these truths.

I became a super self. I became a little bit bolder and more courageous. Paul could confirm that to you if he spoke in one of these interviews. He could tell you how much I matured. I became a better person through the love and guidance of the Holy Spirit, through the revelation that was taught to me. I learned not to fear as much and to speak up and be more courageous in what I had to say.

Question 8:

Paul is remembered in scripture as telling you to take a little wine for your stomach. (See 1 Timothy 5:23.) Was it fermented or unfermented?

You can safely assume that when wine is mentioned in the Bible, it is not talking about unfermented juice. Most of the time, when the Bible mentions wine, it's referring to fermented alcoholic wine. Paul told me in his letter to me to take some fermented wine. Alcohol just helps sometimes with small bugs and issues in your digestive system. Some people would take issue that Paul would suggest the drinking of alcohol. Some people would question why Paul was saying to Timothy to take a bit of wine for stomach bugs rather than believe in divine healing. Some people have real issues with that.

Some healers with powerful healing ministries wear glasses, and their vision hasn't healed. Some people who wear glasses and lead healing ministries heal blind people, and yet their own eyes need glasses. So if you are going to be pedantic about these matters, Paul wasn't. He understood that we have bugs and occasional health issues. A bit of alcohol might have helped. Paul wasn't against alcohol. Jesus turned water into wine after they ran out at a wedding feast after a few days. He certainly wasn't against alcohol. Drinking alcohol can be enjoyable, but some people take it to excess and do damage through the overconsumption of alcohol.

Paul or Jesus do not approve of this, but people have free will and can decide to do things that are contrary to their better judgement. Please understand that Paul wasn't endorsing that people get drunk in that statement to me. But he was certainly recommending the medicinal benefits of alcohol to improve health. People sometimes enjoy wine at dinner with their meal, which Paul encouraged me to do. Like everything Paul said, a lot of thought went into his words, and the Holy Spirit was often behind what he said. You have to weigh yourself and measure your thoughts carefully when you say that the books of the Bible were inspired by the Holy Spirit, and yet that one statement of Paul's wasn't. You'll have to check yourself and see if you're actually right in your assumptions if you don't think it was scriptural or correct.

Question 8:

You were called to come to Paul when he was in prison awaiting martyrdom. Besides the comfort of your friendship, was there

anything important that Paul wanted you to remember when he went to be with God?

Paul had some parting words for me, along with encouragement to keep me happy and to keep me in a good place. (See 1 Timothy 4:1). He spoke a lot about fear and about running my race and living to fulfill my calling on earth. He was reassuring me that he was quite at ease and happy to be martyred, to lose his life. He was just giving me parting words of comfort and love. As I've said, Paul was just amazing and full of love and compassion.

He lived to serve other people and to make them feel accepted, loved, and comfortable. Paul encouraged me. He shared final thoughts and a final bidding goodbye with me, and he mostly encouraged me in those hours before I was taken from him. He was all about me and all about other people. A lot of people assumed that Paul was all about himself and very proud. Paul spoke once in scripture, "For if anyone thinks himself to be something, when he is nothing, he deceives himself." (See Galatians 6:3.) He was very humble, passionate, and zealous, very bold and courageous. Like I've said, he was very loving and compassionate.

His whole life was about ministering the gospel and serving others. Not many people spend time with a person who is so passionate and zealous for the Lord. When you're passionate and zealous for the Lord, life can become pretty lonely because people like to wear Jesus like a handbag—an accessory in their lives. But he isn't the sole focus of their lives. They like to carry Jesus to church like a handbag and put him down during the weekdays at work. They don't live a crucified life where everything they say and do is for Jesus, for his life, and for his gospel. Paul was 100 percent sold out to the gospel of Jesus Christ and his purposes. He was 100 percent sold out to the people who were willing and who were craving the things of God and seeking hard after the knowledge of God.

He was passionate about sowing into people that were hungry for the things of God. Because I was passionate and zealous myself, he made sure to give me some parting words and encouragement. He prayed with me, a beautiful prayer that I still remember today. He commissioned me to go and do good works for the kingdom until I passed on too.

I hope that this has encouraged you. I hope that you've learned something.

I want you to know that God is faithful. He is there for you. If at any time in these interviews, you feel that you don't measure up or you feel as though you aren't doing as well as you could, just understand that God is a compassionate and a loving God, full of grace. He knows where you're at right now. He has the books, the Bible, and the Holy Spirit to help you on your path so that you become a better person and a better Christian. Please don't feel condemned by what the saints say. We've been living in heaven for two thousand years, and we're anointed and in touch with the things of God. Most of us lived a tremendous life on earth, serving our God.

We are passionate about the things of God. Passionate people sometimes make you feel not as worthy and not as good as they are. But this isn't the case. God loves everybody, and he loves you. You're reading this book because God loves you. Be encouraged, press on, and pray for a deeper revelation and a more intimate walk with Jesus Christ, the Savior of the world, and the Lord of lords, the King of kings. Jesus Christ is my Lord and Savior, and he really is a tremendous person to spend a lot of time with, which I do in heaven. God bless you. See you later.

Paul's Comments

This interview was really great as Timothy clearly and simply answered each question. The interview echoed the subject of honor and striving to be like Jesus through the example of Paul. Timothy spoke about the Apostle Paul, expressing how passionate and loving he was, which confirmed the scripture, "Imitate me just as I also imitate Christ." (See 1 Corinthians 11:1.)

Timothy inspired me to write about honor after I realized how he honored his parents by being so grateful to them in this interview. He honors them by speaking so respectfully about them. Matthew also honors his parents when he mentions them in the acknowledgments section of his books.

I believe that the fear of the Lord is a seed for honor. When we fear the Lord, we begin to know about him and learn of his ways, which then leads us to honor him. Many times, when we are young, we don't know about the sacrifices that our parents make for us. We only realize this later, especially when we become adults or parents ourselves. That's when we start to honor and appreciate them.

I challenge you to sit down and count what your parents have done for you and start to honor them. Honor them with your substance or whatever the Lord inspires you to do. You can buy them a gift or have a small family party with your siblings or friends and serve some cake and food and share words of appreciation to your parents. It is not that hard. Perhaps you might honor a guardian or stepparent who has played a significant role in your life. Honor them too. It is the thought that counts, as the saying goes. Use what you have at the inspiration of the Holy Spirit. He also gives small ideas that are great.

I recently read about a student who walked with his great-grandmother when his name was called at graduation to receive his bachelor's degree. He wanted to honor her for being there for him after his mom and grandmother passed on when he was young.

We also need to honor our leaders. The Apostle Paul speaks about honoring our leaders and masters in 1 Timothy 5:17 and 1 Timothy 6:1. You can read more about what God says regarding honor in *Conversations with God: Book 2*. In that book, God spoke to Matthew and said, "The world needs to move in honor. The Christian church needs to know how to set aside their feelings and learn how to honor the leaders I have placed in charge of them. So many people today, including those in my church, have no idea of what honor means." I encourage you to read that book. Timothy highly revered the Apostle Paul and mentioned that he believes every Christian should honor the Apostle Paul simply because of his extensive devotion to Jesus and his dedication to the things of God.

I believe that we can strive to imitate the Apostle Paul as we draw closer to Jesus. These are some of the characteristics of the Apostle Paul that I gleaned from this interview based on Timothy's extensive thoughts:

Passionate
He was devoted to Jesus and on fire with the Holy Spirit for the works of God. In table conversations, he spoke about the gospel.

Loving -
He had no favorites. He loved everyone equally and was very compassionate toward people. Miracles manifested in his eetings.

Patient
Paul could teach anyone from a child to a mature adult, which required a lot of patience as a teacher.

Understanding
Timothy said that Paul could bear with people if they didn't hear him or understand what he was teaching. He would repeat himself or speak in simple terms until they understood his message.

Fearless
Timothy mentioned that Paul was not afraid of anything or anyone. He was not afraid of conflict or of being hurt. He could speak his mind if something was wrong, sinful, or blasphemous.

Courageous

Timothy mentioned many times that he was taught to be courageous and determined, which he likely acquired from the Apostle Paul, who was already displaying these characteristics.

Honorable

Paul had a solid reputation as a spiritual leader; hence Timothy's parents could allow him to take their child under his wing to be mentored by him.

Confident

Timothy mentioned that Paul dressed up professionally, which means he knew the importance of who he was and therefore knew that he had to be well groomed. He confidently dressed for his role.

You can learn more about the Apostle Paul in the interview that Matthew did, *The Apostle Paul Speaks from Heaven*. I hope this interview has touched you as it has moved me. Think of the people who have contributed to your life. You can start with your parents or guardians, whether or not they were there for you. Honor them so that all may go well with you. (See Ephesians 6:2–3.) May God elevate you in life and use you to influence others as you draw close to Jesus. Thank you, and God bless you.

I'd Love to Hear from You

One of the ways that you can bless me as a writer is by writing an honest and candid review of my book on Amazon. I always read the reviews of my books, and I would love to hear what you have to say about this one.

Before I buy a book, I read the reviews first. You can make an informed decision about a book when you have read enough honest reviews from readers. One way to help me sell this book and to give me positive feedback is by writing a review for me. It doesn't cost you a thing but helps me and the future readers of this book enormously.

To read my blog, request a life-coaching session, request your own personal prophecy, or to receive a personal message from your angel, you can also visit my website at *http://personal-prophecy-today.com* All of the funds raised through my ministry website will go toward the books that I write and self-publish.

To write to me about this book or to share any other thoughts, please feel free to contact me at my personal email address at *survivors.sanctuary@gmail.com*

You can also friend request me on Facebook at Matthew Robert Payne. Please send me a message if we have no friends in common as a lot of scammers now send me friend requests.

You can also do me a huge favor and share this book on Facebook as a recommended book to read. This will help me and other readers.

How to Sponsor a Book Project

If you have been blessed by this book, you might consider sponsoring a book for me. It normally costs me between fifteen hundred and two thousand dollars or more to produce each book that I write, depending on the length of the book.

If you seek the Holy Spirit about financing a book for me, I know that the Lord would be eternally grateful to you. Consider how much this book has blessed you and then think of hundreds or even thousands of people who would be blessed by a book of mine. As you are probably aware, the vast majority of my books are ninety-nine cents on Kindle, which proves to you that book writing is indeed a ministry for me and not a money-making venture. I would be very happy if you supported me in this.

If you have any questions for me or if you want to know what projects I am currently working on that your money might finance, you can write to me at *survivors.sanctuary@gmail.com* and ask me for more information. I would be pleased to give you more details about my projects.

You can sow any amount to my ministry by simply sending me money via the PayPal link at this address: *http://personal-prophecy-today.com/support-my-ministry*

You can be sure that your support, no matter the amount, will be used for the publishing of helpful Christian books.

Other Books by Matthew Robert Payne

What I Believe

Living for Eternity

Your Identity in Christ

7 Keys to Intimacy with Jesus

Finding Intimacy with Jesus Made Simple

Finding Your Purpose in Christ

Jesus Speaking Today

His Redeeming Love: A Memoir (Part 2)

The Parables of Jesus Made Simple: Updated and Expanded Edition

Christian Discipleship Made Simple

Nineteen Scriptures to Change Your Life Forever

Influencing your World for Christ: Practical Everyday Evangelism

Optimistic Visions of Revelation

How to Hear God's Voice: Keys to Conversational Two-Way Prayer

Conversations with God: Book 1

Conversations with God: Book 2

Conversations with God: Book 3

Twenty-Two Signs that You're Called to Be a Prophet

Deep Calls unto Deep: Answering Questions on the Prophetic

A Beginner's Guide to the Prophetic

Other Books by Matthew Robert Payne

The Prophetic Supernatural Experience

Prophetic Evangelism Made Simple

My Radical Encounters with Angels

My Radical Encounters with Angels: Book Two

A Message from My Angel: Book 1

Walking under an Open Heaven

My Visits to Heaven: Lessons Learned

Interviews with the Two Witnesses: Enoch and Elijah Speak

Apostle John Speaks from Heaven: A Divine Revelation

Apostle Paul Speaks from Heaven: A Divine Revelation

Apostle Peter Speaks from Heaven: A Divine Revelation

King David Speaks from Heaven: A Divine Revelation

Mary Magdalene Speaks from Heaven: A Divine Revelation

Mary Magdalene Speaks from Heaven Book 2: A Divine Revelation

Great Cloud of Witnesses Speak

Great Cloud of Witnesses Speak: Old and New

Great Cloud of Witnesses Speak: God's Generals

My Visits to the Galactic Council of Heaven

Princess Diana Speaks from Heaven: A Divine Revelation

Michael Jackson Speaks from Heaven

Coping with your Pain and Suffering

Gaining Freedom from Sex Addictions: Breaking Free of Pornography and Prostitutes

Writing and Self-Publishing Christian Nonfiction

Other Books by Matthew Robert Payne

Five Keys to Successful Writing: How I Write One Book per Month

Coming Soon:

Enoch Speaks from Heaven: A Divine Revelation

Be sure to select "Follow" on Matthew Robert Payne's Amazon author page to receive notifications of each new book release. Thank you for your support!

Acknowledgments

Jesus:

I want to thank you for being my lifelong friend and for never deserting me, no matter how dark my life became. You led me into some great adventures.

Holy Spirit:

I want to thank you for leading and teaching me. You are a great teacher, better than I could ever be. You have been with me every step of the way. I thank you for putting it on Paul's heart to transcribe these messages and help me make this book.

Father:

Thank you for loving me and entrusting me with this life that I am living. Thank you for revealing my purpose to me and leading me toward accomplishing it. Thank you so much for your Son, Jesus. Thank you for everything that you have done in my life.

Paul Nthoba:

I want to thank Paul for watching my videos on YouTube and for faithfully selecting four of them and transcribing them and then adding his commentary to the manuscripts. You will receive your reward in heaven for this work.

Lisa Thompson:

I want to give special thanks to Lisa for editing this book of mine. You take my simple words and transform them to make me seem smarter than I really am. If you have any editing needs, Lisa can be contacted at *writebylisa@gmail.com.*

Nicola:

I want to thank Nicola for being part of my team as a proofreader. I want to thank you for all the work that you did with this book to polish and improve it.

Friends:

I want to thank Darla, Lisa, Nicola, Mary, Wendy, Laura, David Joseph, and Michael Van Vlymen for your friendship and for how you have impacted my life.

Mom and Dad:

I want to thank my mother and father for all the love that they have given me. I am a product of your love.

Readers and Ministry Supporters:

I want to thank the readers of my books and my ministry supporters for the funds that you have given me to publish books. I want to thank the man that gave so generously so that I could produce a number of books. I live to educate people, and I thank my readers and the supporters of my ministry because you make life worth living.

About Matthew Robert Payne

Matthew was raised in a Baptist church and was led to the Lord at the tender age of eight. He has experienced some pain and darkness in his life, which have given him a deep compassion and love for all people.

Today, he's a founding member and admin of a Facebook group called "Prophetic Training Group," and he invites you to join him there. Matthew has a commission from the Lord to train up prophets and to mentor others in the Christian faith. He does this through his Facebook posts and by writing relevant books on the Christian faith.

God originally commissioned him to write at least fifty books in his life, but that has now increased to ninety books. He spends his days writing and earning the money to self-publish. You can support him by donating money at *http://personal-prophecy-today.com* or by requesting any of the other services available through his ministry website.

Recently, the Lord has put it on Matthew's heart to start his own publishing company called Christian Book Publishing USA. Matthew hopes to help other people self-publish their books in the future.

Matthew prays that this book has blessed you, and he hopes it will lead you into a deeper and more intimate relationship with God.